The Boy on the Wooden Box

By Leon Leyson

A Complete Novel Study By Jane Kotinek

ISBN-13: 978-1515076933   ISBN-10: 1515076938

Table of Contents

Page	Content
4	**What Does It Mean?** Explanation of symbols used in novel study
5-16	**Vocabulary:** Lists with synonyms, activities, crossword puzzle, and word search
17	**What is a Memoir?**
18-19	**Pre-Reading Task Card Questions**
20	**Background Knowledge Questions Chart**
21	**Character File Activity**
22	**Time Line of Events**
23	**Title Summary Activity**
24-25	**Pictures of Warsaw Ghetto with Writing Activity**
26	**Family Tree Chart Activity**
27-59	**Chapter Analysis:** Questions, Snapshots, Talk About It, Research Ideas
30, 53	**Character Development Activity**
34, 47	**How do the Events Impact the Character? Activity**
38	**Inference Activity**
60	**Character Analysis Essay**
61-66	**Language Arts Activities:** Moment Analyzing Theme, Protagonist vs. Antagonist Activity, Internal vs. External Conflict Chart, Analyzing the Title Activity, Cause and Effect Activity Chart
67-79	**Teacher's Edition:** Answers to Chapter Questions
80-83	**Answers to Vocabulary Activities:** Crossword puzzles, worksheet
84-98	**Assessments:** 4 quizzes and 1 comprehension test
85-86	**Quiz 1 with essay prompt**
87-88	**Quiz 2 with essay prompt**
89-90	**Quiz 3 with essay prompt**
91-92	**Quiz 4 with essay prompt**
93-98	**Comprehension Test with 5 Essay Prompts**
99	**Answers to Assessments**
100	**Credit Given for Clip Art and Borders**

What Do They Mean?

 Snapshot- The "snapshot" should be used as a quick write in an interactive notebook. Snapshots are often used with Reader's Writer's Workshop. The snapshots should be used as quick comprehension assessment tools.

 The "Talk About It" should be used for pair/share or turn-and-talks. They will work great in literature circle groups.

 The magnifying glass illustrates where a research idea is located. These are only suggestions.

 **Visualize It** means the student should draw what they see after reading a specific description.

Copyright © Jane Kotinek All rights reserved by author. This product is to be used by the original downloader only. Copying for more than one teacher, classroom, department, school, or school system is prohibited. This product may not be distributed or displayed digitally for public view. Failure to comply is a copyright infringement and a violation of the Digital Millennium Copyright Act (DMCA). Clipart and elements found in this PDF are copyrighted and cannot be extracted and used outside of this file without permission or license. Intended for classroom and personal use ONLY.

Vocabulary List

The following list contains vocabulary words used in the novel to create tone or mood.

1. anxiety (59) 3
2. brazenly (58) 3
3. chaos (94) 5
4. delirious (121) 7
5. demeaning (52) 3
6. desolation (122) 7
7. despair (124) 7
8. extraordinary (34) 2
9. ferociously (102) 6
10. frantic (59) 3
11. furtively (94) 5
12. futility (100) 6
13. horrific (123) 7
14. impenetrable (90) 5
15. impressive (34) 2
16. jubilant (76) 4
17. rampaged (94) 5
18. shrieks (102) 6
19. squalid (92) 5
20. tumultuous (44) 2

Group 1 List
1. anxiety
2. brazenly
3. demeaning
4. extraordinary
5. frantic
6. impenetrable
7. impressive
8. jubilant
9. squalid
10. tumultuous

Group 2 List
1. chaos
2. delirious
3. desolation
4. despair
5. ferociously
6. furtively
7. futility
8. horrific
9. rampaged
10. shrieks

Words convey different emotions. Some words are stronger, more intense, than other, for instance: horrendous compared to bad. Using the lines provided, rank the vocabulary words from bland to explosive. There are no wrong answers.

1. _____
2. _____
3. _____
4. _____
5. _____
6. _____
7. _____
8. _____
9. _____
10. _____

11. _____
12. _____
13. _____
14. _____
15. _____
16. _____
17. _____
18. _____
19. _____
20. _____

Vocabulary Words

anxiety	to be filled with nervousness, unease, concern
brazenly	to act boldly, blatantly, without care
chaos	confusion, disorder, disruption
delirious	to be ecstatic, extremely happy
demeaning	making one feel inferior by belittling them
desolation	the act of being destroyed, made gloomy, ruin
despair	hopelessness, anguish
extraordinary	amazing, special, odd
ferociously	brutally, violently, cruelly
frantic	desperate, panicky, hysterical
furtively	slyly, secretly, sneakily
futility	pointlessness, uselessness
horrific	horrendous, appalling, horrifying
impenetrable	impassable, solid, unforgiving
impressive	remarkable, striking, outstanding
jubilant	proud, thrilled, delighted
rampaged	rioted, raged, charged
shrieks	yells, screams, screeches
squalid	filthy, nasty, neglected
tumultuous	Violent agitation of mind or feeling. Upheaval

The following table contains the vocabulary words. The synonyms or definition to each word is contained in the right-hand column.

Crossword Puzzle

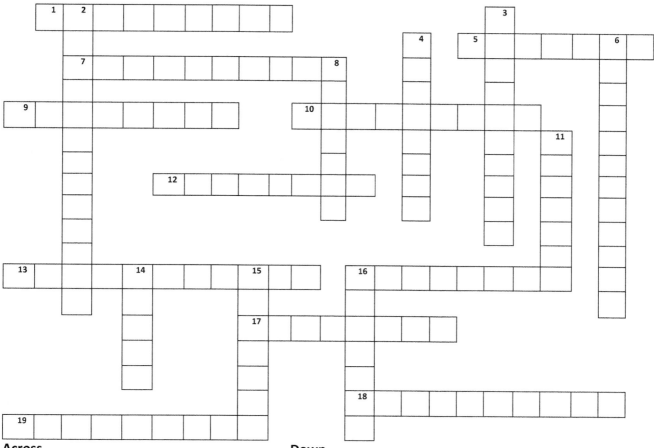

Across

1. making one feel inferior by belittling them
3. the act of being destroyed, made gloomy, ruin
5. hopelessness, anguish
7. violent agitation of mind or feeling. Upheaval
9. to act boldly, blatantly, without care
10. slyly, secretly, sneakily
12. horrendous, appalling, horrifying
13. brutally, violently, cruelly
16. pointlessness, uselessness
17. rioted, raged, charged
18. remarkable, striking, outstanding
19. to be ecstatic, extremely happy

Down

2. amazing, special, odd
4. proud, thrilled, delighted
6. impassable, solid, unforgiving
8. filthy, nasty, neglected
11. to be filled with nervousness, unease, concern
14. confusion, disorder, disruption
15. yells, screams, screeches
16. desperate, panicky, hysterical

Vocabulary Practice (Group 1)

Directions: An example from the book has been provided for each of the vocabulary words. Find a *synonym* for the bold, *italicized* vocabulary word. Rewrite the sentence on the line provided. Does the synonym you used change the meaning or tone of the sentence? Explain your answer.

1. "In this *tumultuous* time I grew ever closer to my brother Tsalig." (Page 44)
   In this unsettling time I grew ever closer to my brother Tsalig.
   The synonym unsettling is not as strong as *tumultuous*. Using it does not change the meaning of the sentence; however, the urgency of the situation is diminished.

2. "As I pulled the chain and watched the water swish against the sides of the bowl, I thought this was about as ***extraordinary*** an invention as there could be." (Page 34)

   Does the meaning change or tone change? Explain your answer.

3. "Pretty soon I felt brave enough to risk exploring on my own. All those scenes I had admired on the candy boxes were even more ***impressive*** in reality." (Page 34)

   Does the meaning change or tone change? Explain your answer.

4. "***Demeaning*** posters appeared in both Polish and German, depicting us as grotesque, filthy creatures, with large, crooked noses." (Page 52)

   Does the meaning change or tone change? Explain your answer.

5. "Because both my brother and I could speak German and because the full villainy of the Germans was not yet evident, we ***brazenly*** questioned every German we thought might know something." (Page 58)

   Does the meaning change or tone change? Explain your answer.

Vocabulary Practice (Group 1)
Page 2

6. "My mother was *frantic*, beseide herself with fear and anxiety." (Page 59)

   _____

   Does the meaning change or tone change? Explain your answer.

   _____

7. "My mother was frantic, beside herself with fear and *anxiety*." (Page 59)

   _____

   Does the meaning change or tone change? Explain your answer.

   _____

8. "I remember going to the empty lot where there was one such screen and watching an endless parade of tanks and *jubilant* German soldiers as they rolled through the Netherlands, Belgium, Luxembourg, and France in May and June of 1940." (Pages 75-76)

   _____

   Does the meaning change or tone change? Explain your answer.

   _____

9. "My father may have been terrified for our safety, but he kept his feelings hidden behind an *impenetrable* expression." (Page 90)

   _____

   Does the meaning change or tone change? Explain your answer.

   _____

©2015 Jane Kotinek All Rights Reserved The Boy On The Wooden Box A Novel Study

Vocabulary Practice (Group 1)
Page 3

10. "Some 1,500 Jews volunteered to go, thinking that anything must be better than the *squalid* environment they were in." (Page 92)

_____

_____

Does the meaning change or tone change? Explain your answer.

_____

_____

Directions: Writer your own sentences using the vocabulary word listed. Do **not** copy the sentences from the book.

11. tumultuous-

12. brazenly-

13. jubilant-

14. squalid-

15. frantic-

16. anxiety-

17. demeaning-

18. extraordinary-

19. impressive-

20. impenetrable-

Vocabulary Practice (Group 2)

Directions: An example from the book has been provided for each of the vocabulary words. Find a *synonym* for the bold, *italicized* vocabulary word. Rewrite the sentence on the line provided. Does the synonym you used change the meaning or tone of the sentence? Explain your answer.

1. "Escapees from earlier deportations had ***furtively*** returned to the ghetto with stories of trains filled with people entering a camp and leaving empty, even though the population of the camp never increased." (Page 94)

   _____

   _____

   Does the meaning change or tone change? Explain your answer.

   _____

   _____

2. "So the next time the Nazis started rounding up Jews, ***chaos*** erupted." (Page 94)

   _____

   _____

   Does the meaning change or tone change? Explain your answer.

   _____

   _____

3. "Soldiers ***rampaged*** through the ghetto, demanding that people show the required identification and shoving anyone who couldn't into the streets teeming with fellow unfortunates." (Page 94)

   _____

   _____

   Does the meaning change or tone change? Explain your answer.

   _____

   _____

4. "Disease spread unchecked, weakening, crippling, and killing indiscriminately. There was an overpowering sense of ***futility***." (Page 100)

   _____

   _____

   Does the meaning change or tone change? Explain your answer.

   _____

   _____

Vocabulary Practice (Group 2)

5. "The German Shepherds used to ferret out people in hiding were barking **ferociously**." (Page 102)

   _____

   _____

   Does the meaning change or tone change? Explain your answer.

   _____

   _____

6. "I covered my ears, trying to block out the **shrieks** and moans and cries of "Please!" and "No!" (Page 102)

   _____

   _____

   Does the meaning change or tone change? Explain your answer.

   _____

   _____

7. "After twenty-five blows I staggered away, **delirious** with pain." (Page 121)

   _____

   _____

   Does the meaning change or tone change? Explain your answer.

   _____

   _____

8. "Driven by pain and **desolation**, that evening I risked additional beatings or worse by sneaking over to my father's barracks." (Page 122)

   _____

   _____

   Does the meaning change or tone change? Explain your answer.

   _____

   _____

9. "The **horrific** days came to follow a routine. We were stunned awake before dawn by the sound of crashing doors and shouted orders." (Page 123)

   _____

   _____

   Does the meaning change or tone change? Explain your answer.

   _____

   _____

Vocabulary Practice (Group 2)

10. "As the months dragged on, I *despaired*. I didn't dare risk trying to see my father or mother again, not because I feared for myself, but because I feared the punishment that would come to them if I were discovered in their barracks." (Page 124)

_____

_____

Does the meaning change or tone change? Explain your answer.

_____

_____

Directions: Writer your own sentences using the vocabulary word listed. Do **not** copy the sentences from the book.

11. chaos-

12. delirious-

13. desolation-

14. despair-

15. ferociously-

16. furtively-

17. futility-

18. horrific-

19. rampaged-

20. shrieks-

Vocabulary Activity 1-

A. anxiety	F. desolation	K. furtively	P. jubilant
B. brazenly	G. despair	L. futility	Q. rampaged
C. chaos	H. extraordinary	M. horrific	R. shrieks
D. delirious	I. ferociously	N. impenetrable	S. squalid
E. demeaning	J. frantic	O. impressive	T. tumultuous

Directions: Write the letter of the vocabulary word in the space next to the correct definition.

1. making one feel inferior by belittling them _____
2. amazing, special, odd _____
3. the act of being destroyed, made gloomy, ruin _____
4. proud, thrilled, delighted _____
5. hopelessness, anguish _____
6. impassable, solid, unforgiving _____
7. violent agitation of mind or feeling. Upheaval _____
8. filthy, nasty, neglected _____
9. to act boldly, blatantly, without care _____
10. to be filled with nervousness, unease, concern _____
11. slyly, secretly, sneakily _____
12. confusion, disorder, disruption _____
13. horrendous, appalling, horrifying _____
14. yells, screams, screeches _____
15. brutally, violently, cruelly _____
16. desperate, panicky, hysterical _____
17. pointlessness, uselessness _____
18. rioted, raged, charged _____
19. remarkable, striking, outstanding _____
20. to be ecstatic, extremely happy _____

Vocabulary Word Search

T	U	M	U	L	T	U	O	U	S	B	U	S	Q	U	A	L	I	D
J	I	A	S	K	E	I	R	H	S	E	Y	T	I	L	I	T	U	F
L	M	M	N	T	O	P	J	E	Y	X	U	J	F	S	F	L	E	D
Y	P	P	N	X	I	M	X	L	I	T	B	X	U	D	A	I	F	U
L	E	C	C	A	I	D	N	B	M	R	L	E	R	E	G	O	D	S
S	N	Y	I	I	X	E	G	U	P	A	G	D	T	S	O	A	H	C
U	E	J	F	M	Z	L	T	J	R	O	N	D	I	O	F	J	L	O
O	T	B	I	A	Y	I	A	Y	E	R	I	E	V	L	L	U	E	S
I	R	A	R	R	J	R	R	G	S	D	N	G	E	A	C	B	U	L
C	A	B	R	E	G	I	Y	P	S	I	A	A	L	T	D	I	F	H
O	B	C	O	S	O	O	U	M	I	N	E	P	Y	I	G	L	X	J
R	L	R	H	S	U	U	S	I	V	A	M	M	R	O	B	A	G	X
E	E	R	I	A	P	S	E	D	E	R	E	A	P	N	H	N	I	H
F	R	A	N	T	I	C	O	U	D	Y	D	R	A	J	C	T	L	K

Directions: Highlight or circle each vocabulary word as you find them in the puzzle. Vocabulary words may be spelled horizontally, backwards, diagonally, or vertically.

ANXIETY	DESOLATION	FURTIVELY	JUBLIANT
BRAZENLY	DESPAIR	FUTILITY	RAMPAGED
CHAOS	EXTRAORDINARY	HORRIFIC	SHRIEKS
DELIRIOUS	FEROCIOUSLY	IMPENETRABLE	SQUALID
DEMEANING	FRANTIC	IMPRESSIVE	TUMULTUOUS

©2015 Jane Kotinek All Rights Reserved The Boy On The Wooden Box A Novel Study

Vocabulary Activity 2

A. anxiety	F. desolation	K. furtively	P. jubilant
B. brazenly	G. despair	L. futility	Q. rampaged
C. chaos	H. extraordinary	M. horrific	R. shrieks
D. delirious	I. ferociously	N. impenetrable	S. squalid
E. demeaning	J. frantic	O. impressive	T. tumultuous

Directions: Write the letter of the vocabulary word in the space next to the correct definition.

1. horrendous, appalling, horrifying _____
2. amazing, special, odd _____
3. slyly, secretly, sneakily _____
4. the act of being destroyed, made gloomy, ruin _____
5. proud, thrilled, delighted _____
6. desperate, panicky, hysterical _____
7. impassable, solid, unforgiving _____
8. violent agitation of mind or feeling. Upheaval _____
9. filthy, nasty, neglected _____
10. to act boldly, blatantly, without care _____
11. to be filled with nervousness, unease, concern _____
12. pointlessness, uselessness _____
13. to be ecstatic, extremely happy _____
14. confusion, disorder, disruption _____
15. making one feel inferior by belittling them _____
16. yells, screams, screeches _____
17. brutally, violently, cruelly _____
18. hopelessness, anguish _____
19. rioted, raged, charged _____
20. remarkable, striking, outstanding _____

What is a Memoir?

A memoir is a form of autobiographical writing about a specific recollection that occurred during a significant event or time period.

A memoir is normally concerned with the personalities or actions from people involved in the event or time period, rather than those of the writer.

An autobiography stresses the private life, actions, and thoughts of the individual who is telling the narrative.

You Try It

Think about the previous year. Was there anything significant about it? Where you somehow connected to it? Describe the event, people involved, and the actions taken. What did you observe or witness during this event? Write about it.

_____
_____
_____
_____
_____
_____
_____
_____
_____
_____
_____
_____
_____
_____
_____
_____
_____

Pre-Reading Task Card Questions

The Boy On The Wooden Box, by Leon Leyson is a thought-provoking story. The reader should come away with additional questions, concerns, and insight. In order to appreciate the story better, I have included pre-reading questions that will help the reader prepare for their literary journey. The amount of questions they answer is up to you, the teacher.

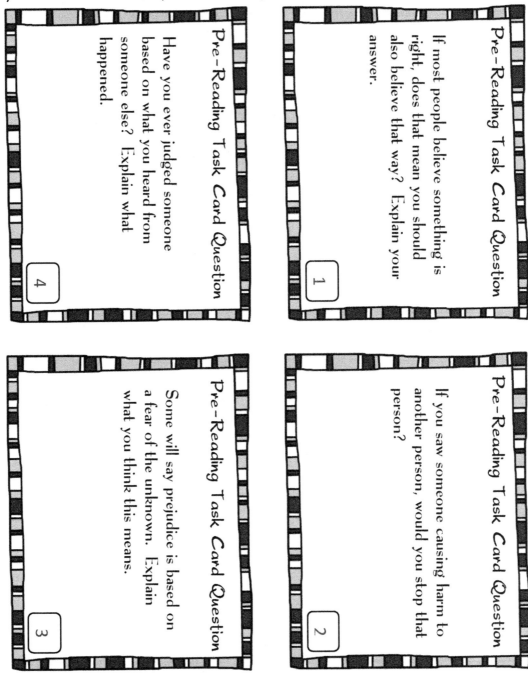

Pre-Reading Task Card Question 1: If most people believe something is right, does that mean you should also believe that way? Explain your answer.

Pre-Reading Task Card Question 2: If you saw someone causing harm to another person, would you stop that person?

Pre-Reading Task Card Question 3: Some will say prejudice is based on a fear of the unknown. Explain what you think this means.

Pre-Reading Task Card Question 4: Have you ever judged someone based on what you heard from someone else? Explain what happened.

Pre-Reading Task Card Question

The extermination of the Jews was horrific. Do you think something like it could occur again? Explain your answer.

5

Pre-Reading Task Card Question

Do you think prejudicial behavior is learned, or does it happen naturally? Explain your answer.

8

Pre-Reading Task Card Question

In your opinion, why do groups of people dislike each other?

6

Pre-Reading Task Card Question

Do you believe it is understandable for people to ignore injustices against others if it means they will not be harmed?

7

Background Knowledge

Directions: Answer the following prompts in the space provided. After answering the questions, discuss your answers with the answers provided by the members of your group. Record, in the space provided, what you thought during and after the discussion with your group.

What do I **know**?	What have I **experienced**?	How do I **react**?
What do I know about prejudice?	How do I define prejudice?	How do I feel about prejudice?
What do I know about the Holocaust?	I have listed specific examples of prejudicial behavior I have read about, seen, or personally experienced.	When I see someone acting in a prejudicial way toward another person, I react by…
Questions I have about the Holocaust…	Questions I have about this…	If I were treated differently because I was of a different race, religion, culture, or gender I would feel…
I learned the following about the Holocaust and prejudices held by people.	This is what my team members experienced…	After the discussion with my group, I feel…
I would like to learn about the following…		

Character Name: _____

Complete each question with a complete sentence.

Where does your character live? _____

Character's age: _____

Describe members of family: _____
_____
_____

What problem is your character having in the story? _____
_____

What does your character look like? (Physical traits) _____

Who are friends of character? _____

What does your character like to do for fun? _____
_____

Where does your character work? _____

What do you want to learn about your character? _____

What changes has your character gone through? _____

What else do you know about your character? _____
_____
_____

Time Line of Events

Keeping track of important events that occur during a story helps the reader visualize and understand the time frame of the events. While you are reading the story, record the major events on the time line. ** You may have to figure out the approximate date of an event if Leon only mentions the months that have passed.

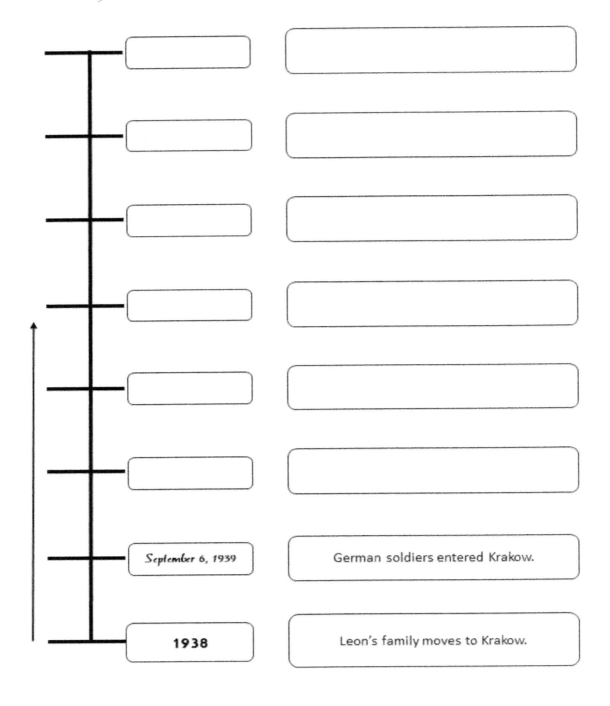

Title Summary Activity

Directions: After reading each chapter, write a title for it that summarizes the key idea of the chapter.

Prologue: _____

Chapter 1: _____

Chapter 2: _____

Chapter 3: _____

Chapter 4: _____

Chapter 5: _____

Chapter 6: _____

Chapter 7: _____

Chapter 8: _____

Chapter 9: _____

Epilogue: _____

Pictures of Warsaw Ghetto

Public Domain Pictures of the Warsaw Ghetto

Public domain picture of the brick fence surrounding the Warsaw Ghetto (above) and Jews being deported from the Warsaw Ghetto (below).
https://commons.wikimedia.org/wiki/File:Ghetto_Wall_Warsaw_Ghetto_010.jpg

Public Domain Picture. Circa 1950 Zbyszko Siemaszko, photographer of Central Photographic Agency (CAF) in Warsaw
https://commons.wikimedia.org/wiki/File:Warsaw_Ghetto_destroyed_by_Germans,_1945.jpg

Reflections About the Pictures

> What did you think about as you looked at the pictures? What emotions did you feel? Write about it.

Family Tree Chart

Directions: Below is a family tree chart. Fill in the names of the children for Moshe and Chanah. In the rectangles under the names, provide as much detail about each child as you can.

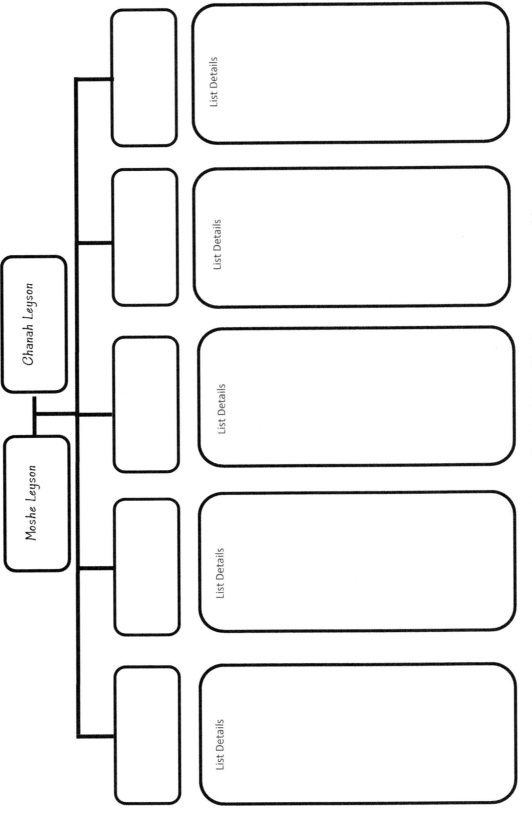

The Boy on the Wooden Box Questions

Prologue

1. Who is Oskar Schindler?

2. Why is it important to understand that people like Oskar Schindler existed during World War II?

 Snapshot: After reading the prologue, what are your thoughts about it? What questions come to your mind?

Chapter 1

1. Describe the setting of Leon's playground when he was young.

2. "After all, I didn't know how to swim." (Page 6) What does this quote say about Leon Leyson?

3. "Life seemed an endless, carefree journey." (Page 7) How does this quote foreshadow the events that will occur?

4. Who is Leib Lejzon?

5. Where was Leon born?

6. Leon's family did not have a lot of money. How did Leon's mother show Leon how proud she was of his hard work?
   _____
   _____

7. Why did Leon's father move to Kraków without his family?
   _____
   _____

8. Why did Leon believe Pesza was his father's favorite child?
   _____
   _____

9. Which sibling did Leon feel closest to?
   _____
   _____

10. Why did Christians treat the Jews differently the week before Easter?
    _____
    _____

11. Explain how the Sabbath was observed by Jews.
    _____
    _____
    _____
    _____

12. What was the *heder*?
    _____
    _____

13. What was the dominate religion in Poland during this time period?

14. Why were the Jews **not** allowed to have a Polish first name?
    _____

15. How does the law prohibiting Jews from owning land in Poland illustrate a form of discrimination?
    _____
    _____
    _____

16. "It was a patriarchal society, in which age was respected, even revered, especially when, as in my maternal grandfather's case, age meant a lifetime of hard work, of caring for his family, and of devotion to his faith." (Page 25) Do you think our society continues to hold this belief? Do you believe the patriarchal society should exist today?
    _____
    _____
    _____
    _____

17. How did Leon's grandfather help the family while Leon's father was away?

18. Describe Leon's relationship with his grandfather.

19. Describe what happened to the men of Poland during the Great War of 1914- 1918.

20. "In retrospect, my parents and many others made a terrible mistake in thinking the Germans who came to Narewka in the Second World War would be like the Germans who had come in the First World War." (Page 28) What can you **infer** from this quote?

Visualize It: Draw a picture, using his description as a guide, of Leon having fun when he was young.

Visualize It: Draw a picture of Narewka. Draw a picture of your town. Explain any differences you notice.

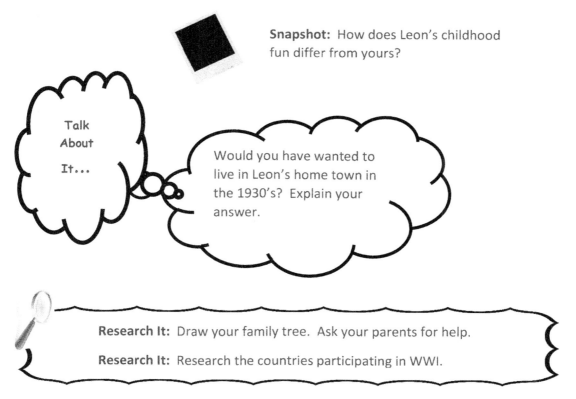

Snapshot: How does Leon's childhood fun differ from yours?

Talk About It...

Would you have wanted to live in Leon's home town in the 1930's? Explain your answer.

Research It: Draw your family tree. Ask your parents for help.

Research It: Research the countries participating in WWI.

Character Development

Characters develop throughout a story. The reader should notice the changes occurring within and outside (physically) of Leon Leyson. These changes are chronicled in his memoir. As good readers, it is our duty to acknowledge these changes and think about the reasons why they were able to occur. You will need to infer a lot of Leon's character traits.

Complete the chart below. You will continue to add to it as you read Leon's story.

Trait	Page	Textual Proof
Rebellious	6	Leon is describing the fun he had at the river during summer. "What made the escapades even more exciting was that my mother had forbidden my going to the river." *Notice how I paraphrased* event before including the textual proof. I did this to supply context (clarity) for the proof.

Chapter 2

1. What did the family give up to achieve their goals of a better life?

2. Describe the culture shock experienced by Lyon when he saw his new home.

3. Why is it important for Leon to mention his non-Jewish friends?

4. How many Jews lived in Kraków? _____

5. How had Hershel changed?

6. "Now, in retrospect, I realize that there were signs pointing to troubled times ahead." (Page 39) What can you infer from this statement?

7. How does Leon's teacher insult him?

8. Why did Hitler hate the Jews?

9. List those things that were happening to Jews in Poland.

10. Why did Leon's parents (and other Jewish parents) downplay the seriousness of what Hitler was doing to them?

11. Explain what happened on November 9-10, 1938 in Germany and Austria.

12. "In fact, much more than glass was shattered that night." (Page 43) What else was shattered?
    _____
    _____

13. Why should the event on November 9-10 been seen as an important turning point for the Jewish people?
    _____
    _____

14. "All of us wanted to believe the bravery of our soldiers could somehow defeat the mighty German military with all its planes and tanks." (Page 44) Why would this be an unrealistic expectation for Poland?
    _____
    _____
    _____
    _____

15. How does Leon's relationship with his brother Tsalig change during this time period?
    _____
    _____

16. How has the atmosphere (mood) of Kraków changed since Leon and his family moved there?
    _____
    _____

17. How did the Jews prepare for the war against Germany?
    _____
    _____

18. Leon's mother expressed concern for her family. "However, without my father's consent and blessing, she would never consider leaving." (Page 46) What can you infer about a woman's place in society during this time period?
    _____
    _____

19. What event happened on September 1, 1939? _____

20. Explain why the males of Poland fled after the invasion.
    _____
    _____
    _____
    _____

21. Where did Leon's father and Herschel decide to go?
    _____
    _____

22. "Without asking my mother's permission, since she surely would not have given it, I sneaked out of our apartment to take a look for myself." (Page 48) What character trait would you give Leon based on this quote? _____

23. How long did it take the German army to reach Kraków? _____

Snapshot: Describe the atmosphere of Kraków in Chapter 2. Provide specific details from the story that supports your opinion.

 Snapshot: What would you be willing to give up to attain your goals?

 Snapshot: What do you think will happen to Leon's father and brother?

How do the Events Impact the Character?

Major events occur in the story. These events impact the characters (either positively or negatively). Complete the diagram as you (the reader) encounter these events. Explain how the event impacts (affects) the character.

Event
Describe the event

Circle whether it is a positive or negative event.

Explain the impact the event had on the character.

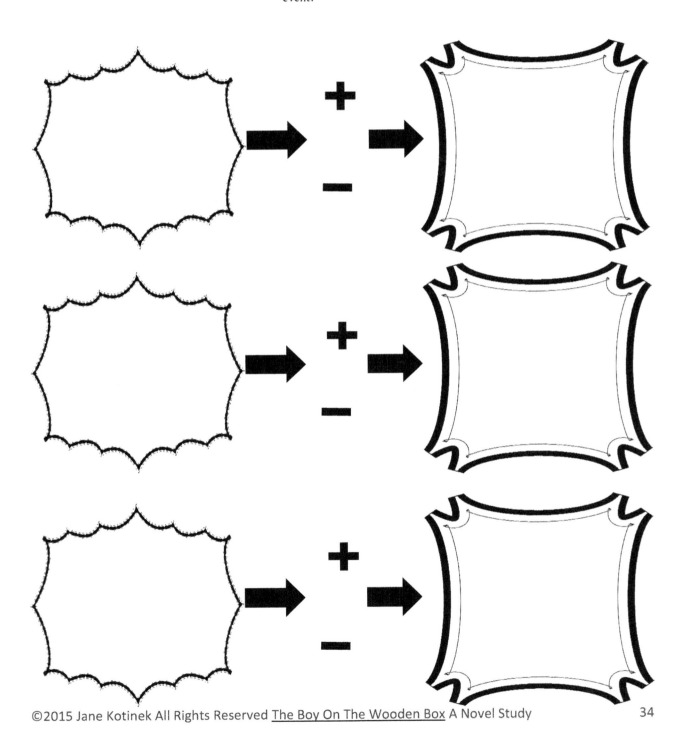

©2015 Jane Kotinek All Rights Reserved The Boy On The Wooden Box A Novel Study

Chapter 3

1. Why did Hershel continue on to Narewka?

2. Why do you think the German's depicted Jews the way they did?

3. Explain the restrictions placed on Jews by Hitler.

4. How did Leon's relationship with his non-Jewish friends change?

5. Explain how the Jews were treated by the German soldiers.

6. How did Leon's father's skills save the family?

7. Why did Leon's father believe the war would not last long?

8. "My father was making the same mistake so many others were, believing that the Germans with whom he was now dealing were no different from the ones he had known before. He had no idea, nor could he have had, of the limitless inhumanity and evil of this new enemy." (Page 55) Do you think Leon is exaggerating the situation? What signs were present in Kraków that should have alerted Leon's father of the danger they were about to face?

9. Explain what happened to Leon's father after the soldiers broke into their apartment.
   _____
   _____

10. Explain how the events from the night the soldiers broke into Leon's apartment became "the symbol for all the horrible viciousness that would follow." (Page 57)
    _____
    _____
    _____
    _____

11. How was Leon and his family able to survive while his father was missing?
    _____
    _____
    _____
    _____

12. What was Leon no longer allowed to attend? _____
13. Where was Leon's father? _____
14. What did Leon's father lose while he was in prison?
    _____
    _____

15. Why do you think Jews were required to wear the Star of David on their clothes?
    _____
    _____

16. How did Leon resist the decrees? Do you think he should have taken the risk?
    _____
    _____

17. Describe how Leon has changed.
    _____
    _____
    _____
    _____

18. Why did the Nazi offer a job to Leon's father?
    _____
    _____

19. Why did Leon's father take the job offered to him?
    _____
    _____

20. Who was the owner of the factory? _____

Snapshot: Why did non-Jews treat the Jews the way they did? Do you believe they had a right to treat them so badly?

Snapshot: Can you imagine living in the conditions Leon and his family were subjected to? What would you do differently? What risks would you be willing to take (knowing a consequence could be death)?

Talk About It...

"Maybe, beaten down as he already was and ready to grab on to the thinnest lifeline of hope, he just thought, *Do as you're told. Don't make trouble. Show your value. Survive.*" How would following this train of thought save a Jews life?

Research It: What is propaganda? What is the purpose of it? Does your country use it? Explain your answers.

Inference Activity

Inference- to make a *logical* **guess** *based* on the **clues** provided in the text and your background knowledge.

In the chart below, record the inferences you had to make while reading the novel. You should record the sentence(s) from the novel, the page number where you found the quote, and the inference you made.

Quote from Novel	Page Number	Inference
I always stood a little taller and felt a little more special when people spoke of me as Jacob Meyer's *eynikl*.	25	There are 2 inferences that may be made from this example. Leon is very proud of his grandfather. His grandfather is very respected in the community (otherwise, why would Leon stand taller when people spoke of his grandfather?).

Chapter 4

1. Describe Oskar Schindler and his business practices.

2. Explain why being employed was so important for a Jew?

3. What is a *Bescheinigung*?

4. What did Leon do almost daily since he did not have to wear the Star of David and he did not look Jewish?

5. Explain why Leon's actions with the German soldiers is ***ironic***.

6. Describe the "cleansing" that took place in Kraków in May 1940.

7. How must the Jews have felt during this time?

8. "They told us the departing Jews were going to better lives away from the city, where they would be in less crowded conditions and not have to endure the relentless harassment from German soldiers patrolling the streets." (Page 73) Given the treatment toward Jews by the German soldiers, was it wise for the Jews to believe them? What choices did they have if they chose not to believe what was being told to them?

9. What risks did Leon's father take in an attempt to help his family?

_____
_____
_____
_____

10. What was the name of the new ghetto in Poland? _____

11. "I watched as twelve-foot-high walls went up, encircling an area of residential buildings not far from our apartments. The Nazis then ordered 5,000 non-Jews living within the area to move out so that 15,000 Jews- every Jew still in Kraków- could be crammed into these new quarters." (Pages 76-77) How does this description set the mood for Podgórze? What kind of life should the Jews expect after moving into the new ghetto?

_____
_____
_____
_____

12. Why did the rounded stones on the walls symbolize a cemetery for the Jews living in Podgórze?

_____
_____

13. Who shared the apartment with Leon and his family?

_____

14. What did the Nazis do after the 15,000 Jews were relocated to the ghetto?

_____

15. How do humans cope with extreme situations?

_____
_____

Visualize It: Draw a picture using the description on page 76.

Snapshot: You may have heard that stealing is never right. Do you think Leon's father had the right to steal food and coal from his workplace? Explain your answer.

Snapshot: "If this is the worst that happens." Why would Jewish parents consider this a tool of survival?

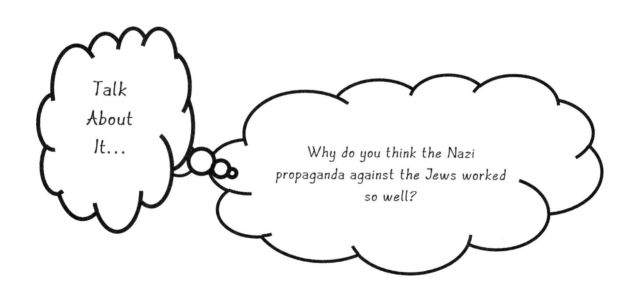

Talk About It...

Why do you think the Nazi propaganda against the Jews worked so well?

Chapter 5

1. Why did Mr. Luftig's pipes symbolize an orderly and civilized world?

2. What were the causes of the rampant diseases within the ghetto?

3. How do you think the Nazis justified their actions against the Jews?

4. How did the Jews sustain their respect and decency toward one another?

5. How did Leon spend his free time in the ghetto?

6. How did Leon's family get money for food?

7. Describe how each member of the family contributed to their survival.

8. What explanation does Leon give for the reason why his family did not make plans for the future?

9. Explain the meaning of a "nonessential" Jew.

10. What should you have inferred about Mr. Luftig leaving his pipes behind?

11. Why did the Jews react differently during the next round of evictions?

12. Describe what happened to Tsalig.

Snapshot: Imagine thinking one piece of bread was a treat. What thoughts run through your mind when you think of a treat?

Talk About It...

Oskar Schindler recounts seeing Tsalig. Why do you think Tsalig decided to stay with his girlfriend? What does that say about him? Do you think he made a good choice?

Chapter 6

1. What happened to Leon when he was out past curfew?

2. Describe the conditions in the ghetto.

3. What strategy did Leon's mother and Mrs. Bircz devise to protect them from deportation?

4. Do you think their strategy was a good idea?

5. Explain why the teapot being in the courtyard was a horrible mistake?

6. Why did they not come out of hiding after the person said it was safe to do so?

7. "Yossel and Samuel would have to rely on their own resources." (Page 105) What does Leon mean with this statement?

8. Where were Leon's father, brother and sister ordered to report?

9. What was significant about the orders?

10. Why did Leon's mother push all their furniture over the balcony?

11. Why was Leon pulled from the work line?

12. How did Leon manage to get through the gate to Ghetto A?

13. What astonished Leon when he walked through the streets of Kraków?

14. "Stepping through those gates was like arriving at the innermost circle of hell." (Page 112) Explain what you think Leon meant.

Snapshot: What does Leon mean when he states, "By this time survival was mostly a matter of pure luck"?

Snapshot: Explain how you feel after reading the description of Leon hiding from the soldiers. What thoughts went through your mind? Could you imagine living in constant fear?

Snapshot: Leon writes about not knowing if each day would be the last day he would see his mother. What does this make you think about?

Talk About It... Discuss what it must have been like to lose your entire family. What would you do to survive? Given the situation in the ghetto, would you give up or fight for your survival?

Talk About It... How do you think the people living in Kraków were able to distance themselves to what was going on in the ghetto? Do you believe they really did not know the horrors of the ghettos?

Research It: Research Plaszów. What was its purpose?

How do the Events Impact the Character?

Major events occur in the story. These events impact the characters (either positively or negatively). Complete the diagram as you (the reader) encounter these events. Explain how the event impacts (affects) the character.

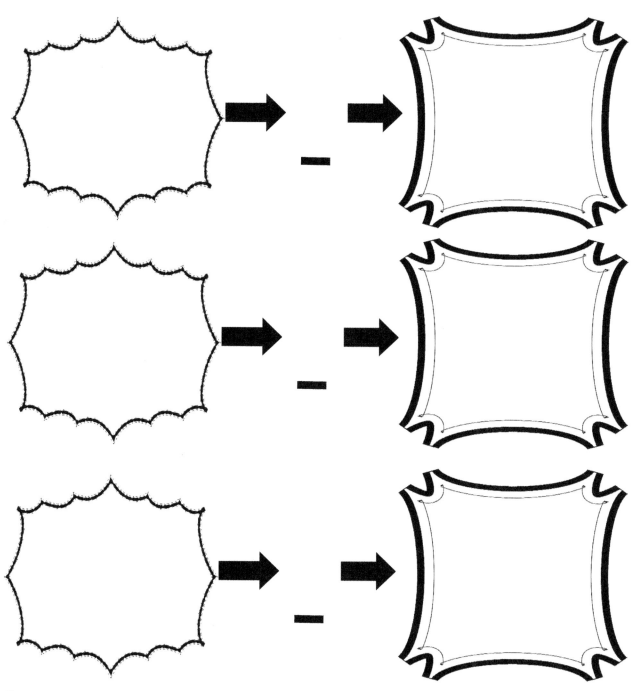

Chapter 7

1. How was Plaszów an insult to all Jews?

2. Describe the conditions at Plaszów.

3. Leon relates visiting his mother in her barracks. Why did she push him away?

4. Like most of the Jews, Leon's family was scattered everywhere. Explain how you would cope if you were in a similar situation.

5. What did SS Hauptsturmführer Amon Goeth do when he visited the infirmary?

6. Why do you think Leon's father did not respond to Leon's story of being whipped?

7. How did the prisoners ladling the soup make Leon's day exceptional?

8. Why did Leon believe he was lucky to have a job in the brush factory?

9. "If the next brad is crooked, I'll shoot you, he said." (Pages 126-27) What does this quote say about the character of the soldier?

10. "I had grown numb to what might happen to me, to whatever my fate might be." (Page 127) Explain what Leon means.

11. How was Schindler able to convince Goeth to build a sub-camp next to Emalia?

12. When Leon finds out he is to be kept at Plaszów, he states, "No words can express the absolute terror I felt. Having been given a little ray of hope, the loss of it was worse than not having had it all." What does he mean?

_____
_____
_____
_____

13. Leon has written about the risks he has taken. Do you think the risks were worth it? Explain your answer.

_____
_____
_____
_____

14. Why do you think the soldier allowed Leon to join the group of workers leaving for the sub-camp?

_____
_____

15. What would have happened to Leon if he had stayed at Plaszów?

_____
_____

Visualize It: Using the description from pages 113-114, draw Plaszów as you see it in your mind.

Snapshot: After reading about the conditions of Plaszów, how do you think the Jews managed to retain hope? How were they able to not give up?

Snapshot: After reading about Leon's ordeal on pages 120–121, explain the emotions you found yourself thinking.

Snapshot: Imagine yourself as Leon as Goeth debated what to do with the two groups of Jews. How would you react?

Talk About It…

How did soldiers justify (reason) their abhorrent treatment of other humans?

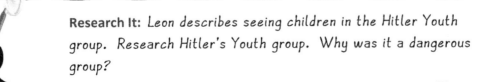

Research It: Leon describes seeing children in the Hitler Youth group. Research Hitler's Youth group. Why was it a dangerous group?

Chapter 8

1. "I knew from experience that invisibility was the closest I could get to safety." (Page 134) What does Leon mean when he talks about being invisible?

2. Describe the differences between Emalia and Plaszów.

3. How did Schindler treat the Jews?

4. Leon writes of proudly telling Schindler he made twelve casings a night. He later found out that a skilled worker made twice as many. What does this exchange say about Schindler?

5. "Schindler dared to rebel against the law of the land, which was to torture and exterminate Jews, not to treat us as fellow human beings. To do that was to risk imprisonment in a labor or concentration camp or execution." (Pages 141-42) Explain why Schindler took the risks he did to protect the Jews in his factory.

6. Why did Germany begin to lose the war?

7. "When we found out German businessmen were packing their bags, leaving their factories, and fleeing Kraków with as much money as many valuables as they could carry, we knew Germany was truly losing the war." (Page 144) Why would this news not be celebrated by the Jews?

8. Why did Leon's father have faith Schindler would be able to save them?

9. How was Leon able to save himself, his father, and his brother from being sent back to Plaszów?

10. Explain how the Germans were trying to hide the atrocities they had committed?
_____
_____

Snapshot: Leon described many incidences where a Jew's life depended on the whim of a soldier. What psychological effect would this complete control have on a person?

Snapshot: The Jews were packed into cattle cars to be sent to different camps. How does this treatment illustrate how the Germans felt about the Jews?

Talk About It... Of all of the things that happened to Leon and his family, what do you think was the worst?

Character Development

Complete the chart below. Do not use traits you have already listed.

Trait	Page	Textual Proof

Chapter 9

1. How did the accommodations at the new factory compare to Gross-Rosen?

2. Why was Leon's father distressed when he heard the train carrying the females had gone to Auschwitz?

3. How did Schindler manage to get the women out of Auschwitz?

4. Schindler spent a lot of his money trying to save the Jews. What does this say about his character?

5. What was surprising about the munition factory?

6. How was Leon able to get scraps from the kitchen help?

7. What affect did the transfer to day shift have on Leon?

8. Explain why the factory workers were not optimistic about the end of the war.

9. How did Schindler save the factory workers in April 1945?

10. How did the German soldiers show themselves to be cowards?

11. Why did Schindler ask the factory workers to not take revenge on the nearby town?

Snapshot: How do you think people can convince themselves that a group of people are less than human?

 Snapshot: Why did the Jews not leave the factory?

Talk About It... Why would the Jews have a hard time comprehending the fact that they were free?

Talk About It... More than 6 million people were exterminated by the Nazis. Oskar Schindler had saved almost 1,200 Jews. Why was Schindler's accomplishment considered an extraordinary feat?

Chapter 10

1. Why did Leon want to remember the German soldiers walking past him?

2. "Trees sprouted new leaves; wildflowers were blooming." (Page 168) What does this symbolize for Leon?

3. How were the Jews treated when they returned to Kraków?

4. Why did people in Kraków not welcome the Jews home?

5. Describe the treatment of Jews in Kraków after they returned?

6. What happened to Leon's family in Narewka?

7. What had happened to Hershel?

8. How did Wetzlar differ from the other camps Leon had been in?

9. Why was it important for the Jews to have the worse story?

10. How did Leon know Dr. Neu had retained his humanity during the war?

11. What did Leon's fedora hat symbolize to him?

Snapshot: What did you find startling about the number of Jews living in Kraków pre-war and after the war?

 Snapshot: What, if anything, did we learn about ourselves from the events of WWII?

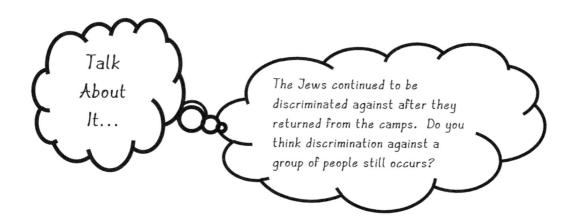

Epilogue

1. "He had no clue of the difference between what he had experienced in having only small quantities of butter and meat during the war and what I had experienced scrounging through garbage searching for a potato peel." (Page 186) Do you think most people would have a difficult time comprehending the hunger Leon went through during the war? Explain your answers.

   _____
   _____
   _____
   _____

2. Explain how Leon was able to make a better life for himself in America.

   _____

3. Why did Leon flash back to the treatment of Jews after having the bus driver tell him he could not sit in the seat on the bus?

   _____
   _____
   _____

4. Explain how Schindler constantly showed his humanity through his actions during the war. Use specific examples.

   _____
   _____
   _____
   _____
   _____
   _____

5. Explain what Campbell meant when he said heroes do "the best of things in the worst of times". (Page 205)

   _____
   _____
   _____
   _____

Snapshot: Do you think it was fair of Leon to compare the two types of discrimination? Explain your answer.

 Snapshot: "To many of his fellow Germans, Schindler had been a traitor to his country, a "Jew lover." (Page 196) Do you think this was a fair portrayal of Schindler? Explain your answer.

 Snapshot: What would be your definition of a hero?

Character Analysis

It is important to think about and try to understand the characters we read about, because their actions and behaviors can provide us, the reader, with insight to our own behavior. In this exercise, you should revisit the lists you made about Leon's character traits. Write an essay explaining the changes Leon went through. Think about the type of person Leon was and the person he became. Write a well-organized essay explaining how you see Leon.

Language Arts Activities

(Answers NOT provided)

Analyzing Theme

Directions: Discuss the themes of the story after you have completed answering the questions below. There are numerous themes in this story.

Theme: A **general idea** or message the author is trying to relay to the reader. A theme is normally concerned with life, human nature, or society. A theme is a universal idea that is usually not stated (implicit) rather than directly stated (explicit). It is understood by the reader through evidence presented in the storyline. A theme is normally written as a complete sentence. (**Basic** examples of theme: love vs. hate (love conquers all), loyalty vs. disloyalty, fairness, and overcoming obstacles.)

1. Brainstorm as many themes as you can for this story. Write them below.
   _____
   _____
   _____

2. Which theme idea do you feel is the most important to the story? Explain your answer.
   _____
   _____
   _____

3. What evidence from the story supports your claim of the most important theme?
   _____
   _____
   _____

4. What message do you think the author wanted you learn after reading his story?
   _____
   _____
   _____

5. What other theme do you believe runs through this story? Why?
   _____
   _____
   _____

Protagonist vs. Antagonist

Directions: Complete the charts below. Use textual proof from the story you are reading to support the traits and actions you list. Remember, the protagonist and/or antagonist does *not* need to be a human.

Protagonist _____

Traits	Textual Proof
Actions	

Antagonist: _____

Traits	Textual Proof
Actions	

Internal/External Conflicts

Directions: There are many conflicts occurring within the story. Complete the chart below to demonstrate your understanding of the conflicts taking place in the novel. Put your choice of a conflict occurring in the story in the last box. An **external conflict** is a problem caused from outside the person (hurricane, tornado, or assassin). An **internal conflict** is a problem the character has within themselves (low self-esteem, obesity, shyness).

Conflict	Explanation of Conflict
Leon vs. himself	
The Jews vs. _____	
_____ **vs.** _____	

Analyzing the Title Activity

Directions: An author chooses the title of their novel for a specific reason. Evaluate the title of the novel and explain why it is or is not a good title.

1. Does the title have a specific meaning to the book? If so, what is the meaning?

   _____

   _____

   _____

   _____

2. In the case of this novel, who or what does the title apply to?

   _____

   _____

3. Create a different title for the novel. Why do you think your title would/would not be a better title?

   _____

   _____

4. Comparing your title with the original, why is the original title better or worse than your choice?

   _____

   _____

   _____

   _____

Cause and Effect Activity

Directions: Complete the cause and effect relationships listed below.

Cause	Effect
Leon's family moves to Kraków.	Leon is exposed to new technology. His family is also in the city when the German soldiers enter it.

Essay Question: Explain how the cause/effect relationships move the story along.

_____
_____
_____
_____
_____
_____
_____
_____
_____

Teacher's Edition

The Boy on the Wooden Box Questions

Prologue

1. Who is Oskar Schindler? **Oskar Schindler helped save over 1200 Jews from dying during Hitler's reign.**
2. Why is it important to understand that people like Oskar Schindler existed during World War II? **People like Schindler proved that humanity still existed. The horrors of the atrocities against those Hitler deemed undesirable showcased the great lengths people like Schindler went through to protect a few of the targeted, even at their own peril.**

Snapshot: After reading the prologue, what are your thoughts about it? What questions come to your mind?

Chapter 1

1. Describe the setting of Leon's playground when he was young. **Leon describes a beautiful, carefree place filled with innocence and fun.**
2. "After all, I didn't know how to swim." (Page 6) What does this quote say about Leon Leyson? **It shows he is a risk taker. It also shows he acts impulsively, without careful thought to any consequences that may occur to him.**
3. "Life seemed an endless, carefree journey." (Page 7) How does this quote foreshadow the events that will occur? **Leon was about to embark on a life that was not carefree. His life would become a dramatic, life-threatening journey.**
4. Who is Leib Lejzon? **Leon Leyson**
5. Where was Leon born? **He was born in Narewka, Poland.**
6. Leon's family did not have a lot of money. How did Leon's mother show Leon how proud she was of his hard work? **She made him scrambled eggs.**
7. Why did Leon's father move to Kraków without his family? **He did not have enough money to move his family with him.**
8. Why did Leon believe Pesza was his father's favorite child? **She was the only girl (besides his mother) in the family.**
9. Which sibling did Leon feel closest to? **Leon felt closest to his brother David.**
10. Why did Christians treat the Jews differently the week before Easter? **Christians viewed the Jews as "Christ killers" during this week.**
11. Explain how the Sabbath was observed by Jews. **Shops and businesses were closed so the Jewish community to celebrate the Sabbath from Friday night to sunset Saturday. The congregation would gather together.**
12. What was the *heder*? **It was a Jewish school where Hebrew and the study of the bible took place.**
13. What was the dominate religion in Poland during this time period? **Roman Catholicism.**
14. Why were the Jews **not** allowed to have a Polish first name? **It was against the law.**
15. How does the law prohibiting Jews from owning land in Poland illustrate a form of discrimination? **Answers will vary. Answers should include something to the effect of a group**

of people do not share the same rights and privileges of others based on their religious affiliation.

16. "It was a patriarchal society, in which age was respected, even revered, especially when, as in my maternal grandfather's case, age meant a lifetime of hard work, of caring for his family, and of devotion to his faith." (Page 25) Do you think our society continues to hold this belief? Do you believe the patriarchal society should exist today? **Answers will vary.**
17. How did Leon's grandfather help the family while Leon's father was away? **He provided them with food.**
18. Describe Leon's relationship with his grandfather. **Leon respected his grandfather very much. Leon sought his grandfather's approval.**
19. Describe what happened to the men of Poland during the Great War of 1914- 1918. **The men were forced to work for the Germans. At the end of the war, the men returned home.**
20. "In retrospect, my parents and many others made a terrible mistake in thinking the Germans who came to Narewka in the Second World War would be like the Germans who had come in the First World War." (Page 28) What can you **infer** from this quote? **The Jews of Poland will be treated very badly in the new occupation.**

Visualize It: Draw a picture, using his description as a guide, of Leon having fun when he was young.

Visualize It: Draw a picture of Narewka. Draw a picture of your town. Explain any differences you notice.

Snapshot: How does Leon's childhood fun differ from yours?

Talk About It: Would you have wanted to live in Leon's home town in the 1930's? Explain your answer.

Research It: Draw your family tree. Ask your parents for help.

Research It: Research the countries participating in WWI.

Chapter 2

1. What did the family give up to achieve their goals of a better life? **Their father had to be away from his family for years. The family had to move from the only village they knew to a strange, crowded city.**
2. Describe the culture shock experienced by Lyon when he saw his new home. **Their apartment had two rooms. They had to share the bathroom with three other families. Their apartment building had indoor plumbing and electricity.**
3. Why is it important for Leon to mention his non-Jewish friends? **He wanted to show how normal his life was after he first moved to Kraków. People of different religions got along.**
4. How many Jews lived in Kraków? **60,000**
5. How had Hershel changed? **He had matured while living in Kraków. He had become considerate, responsible, and hard-working.**
6. "Now, in retrospect, I realize that there were signs pointing to troubled times ahead." (Page 39) What can you infer from this statement? **The Third Reich will begin passing laws against Jews.**
7. How does Leon's teacher insult him? **Leon's teacher insulted him by calling him Mosiek or "little Moses".**
8. Why did Hitler hate the Jews? **He blamed them for all of Germany's troubles.**

9. List those things that were happening to Jews in Poland. **1. 17,000 Jews were thrown out of Germany. 2. Discrimination against Jews increased. 3. Poland refused to allow the 17,000 Jews to enter Poland.**
10. Why did Leon's parents (and other Jewish parents) downplay the seriousness of what Hitler was doing to them? **Answers may vary. Parents were trying to protect their children. They hoped the changes would not last.**
11. Explain what happened on November 9 -10, 1938 in Germany and Austria. **The *Kristallnacht* (the Night of Broken Glass) occurred. Jewish businesses were destroyed along with synagogues and Torah scrolls. Jews were beaten and murdered.**
12. "In fact, much more than glass was shattered that night." (Page 43) What else was shattered? **The hopes, dreams, and spirits of the Jewish community were also destroyed.**
13. Why should the event on November 9-10 been seen as an important turning point for the Jewish people? **Answers will vary. Their situation would only get worse. Their lives would be destroyed by Hitler.**
14. "All of us wanted to believe the bravery of our soldiers could somehow defeat the mighty German military with all its planes and tanks." (Page 44) Why would this be an unrealistic expectation for Poland? **Germany was too strong. Poland did not have a strong enough army to defend itself from Germany.**
15. How does Leon's relationship with his brother Tsalig change during this time period? **Leon becomes closer to his brother.**
16. How has the atmosphere (mood) of Kraków changed since Leon and his family moved there? **It has become more dangerous and unfriendly. The family has become worried about the events occurring in Poland against the Jewish community.**
17. How did the Jews prepare for the war against Germany? **They saved whatever they could (food, money); they remodeled their bomb shelters; and they left Poland.**
18. Leon's mother expressed concern for her family. "However, without my father's consent and blessing, she would never consider leaving." (Page 46) What can you infer about a woman's place in society during this time period? **Women were expected to stay with their husband and obey them.**
19. What event happened on September 1, 1939? **Germany invaded Poland.**
20. Explain why the males of Poland fled after the invasion. **The men did not want to be conscripted into the German army as forced laborers. The men assumed the women and children would not be bothered by the German army.**
21. Where did Leon's father and Herschel decide to go? **They would go back to Narewka.**
22. "Without asking my mother's permission, since she surely would not have given it, I sneaked out of our apartment to take a look for myself." (Page 48) What character trait would you give Leon based on this quote? **Irresponsible, risk-taker, curious**
23. How long did it take the German army to reach Kraków? **6 days**

Essay Question: Describe the atmosphere of Kraków in Chapter 2. Provide specific details from the story that supports your opinion.

Snapshot: What would you be willing to give up to attain your goals?

Snapshot: What do you think will happen to Leon's father and brother?

Talk About It: What do you think Leon and his family should do now that Germany is in Poland?

Chapter 3

1. Why did Hershel continue on to Narewka? **Herschel was young and strong. He stood a better chance of surviving than his father.**
2. Why do you think the German's depicted Jews the way they did? **They wanted non-Jews to be afraid of them. The German's wanted the Jews to be hated by everyone.**
3. Explain the restrictions placed on Jews by Hitler. **They could not sit on park benches or go to the parks. They were told where to sit on buses. Eventually, they were not allowed to use public transportation.**
4. How did Leon's relationship with his non-Jewish friends change? **They started to ignore him. They started to say mean words at him. They would not play with him.**
5. Explain how the Jews were treated by the German soldiers. **The soldiers stole from their stores and homes. They evicted the Jews from their homes. They beat them.**
6. How did Leon's father's skills save the family? **The factory where he worked was owned by a Jew. The Nazis took it. The new owner kept Leon's father working there.**
7. Why did Leon's father believe the war would not last long? **Answers will vary. He probably hoped it would not last long.**
8. "My father was making the same mistake so many others were, believing that the Germans with whom he was now dealing were no different from the ones he had known before. He had no idea, nor could he have had, of the limitless inhumanity and evil of this new enemy." (Page 55) Do you think Leon is exaggerating the situation? What signs were present in Kraków that should have alerted Leon's father of the danger they were about to face? **Answers will vary.**
9. Explain what happened to Leon's father after the soldiers broke into their apartment. **He was beaten and dragged out of the apartment.**
10. Explain how the events from the night the soldiers broke into Leon's apartment became "the symbol for all the horrible viciousness that would follow." (Page 57) **Leon had thought he and his family was safe because his father worked in the factory. He now realized they were not safe. Anything could happen to any Jew living in Kraków.**
11. How was Leon and his family able to survive while his father was missing? **They used the hidden gold coins to buy food. Leon, David, and Pesza got jobs that allowed them to get a little bit of food.**
12. What was Leon no longer allowed to attend? **He was no longer allowed to attend school.**
13. Where was Leon's father? **His father was at St. Michael's prison.**
14. What did Leon's father lose while he was in prison? **He lost his dignity, confidence, self-esteem, strength, and job.**
15. Why do you think Jews were required to wear the Star of David on their clothes? **It was another way to humiliate the Jews. They could also be recognized easier as Jews.**
16. How did Leon resist the decrees? Do you think he should have taken the risk? **Leon would sit on the forbidden park benches.**
17. Describe how Leon has changed. **Answers will vary. He has become more resourceful and mature. His innocence has been destroyed.**
18. Why did the Nazi offer a job to Leon's father? **His father had broken into a safe for the owner of the factory.**

19. Why did Leon's father take the job offered to him? **It would provide a little safety to the family.**
20. Who was the owner of the factory? **Oskar Schindler**

Research It: What is propaganda? What is the purpose of it? Does your country use it? Explain your answers.

Snapshot: Why did non-Jews treat the Jews like they did? Do you believe they had a right to treat them so badly?

Snapshot: Can you imagine living in the conditions Leon and his family have been subjected to? What would you do differently? What risks would you be willing to take (knowing a consequence could be death)?

Talk About It: "Maybe, beaten down as he already was and ready to grab on to the thinnest lifeline of hope, he just thought, *Do as you're told. Don't make trouble. Show your value. Survive.*" How would following this train of thought save a Jews life?

Chapter 4

1. Describe Oskar Schindler and his business practices. **Schindler bought a business from a bankrupt Jewish businessman. Schindler's company produced enamelware pots and pans for Germans. He used Polish workers because he did not have to pay them much. He did not have to pay Jews at all.**
2. Explain why being employed was so important for a Jew? **If a Jew were employed they could not be made to do forced labor (as long as he/she showed the necessary credentials). Jews could also manage to hide away small amounts of food they received or found in the factory.**
3. What is a *Bescheinigung*? **It was a document stating a Jew was officially employed by a German company.**
4. What did Leon do almost daily since he did not have to wear the Star of David and he did not look Jewish? **He kept company with German soldiers. They would talk to each other. The soldiers invited Leon into their guard house and shared bits of chocolate with him.**
5. Explain why Leon's actions with the German soldiers is ironic. **He was a Jew. The German soldiers were supposed to hate him. Instead, not realizing he was a Jew, they were nice to him.**
6. Describe the "cleansing" that took place in Kraków in May 1940. **Tens of thousands of Jews were deported from Kraków. Only 15,000 Jews were allowed to remain in Kraków.**
7. How must the Jews have felt during this time? **Answers will vary. Answers should include some of the following: angry, afraid, scared, worried, resentful**
8. "They told us the departing Jews were going to better lives away from the city, where they would be in less crowded conditions and not have to endure the relentless harassment from German soldiers patrolling the streets." (Page 73) Given the treatment toward Jews by the German soldiers, was it wise for the Jews to believe them? What choices did they have if they chose not to believe what was being told to them? **Answers will vary.**
9. What risks did Leon's father take in an attempt to help his family? **Leon's father took his food home instead of eating it. When the weather became cold, he took coal from the factory furnaces.**

10. What was the name of the new ghetto in Poland? **Podgórze**
11. "I watched as twelve-foot-high walls went up, encircling an area of residential buildings not far from our apartments. The Nazis then ordered 5,000 non-Jews living within the area to move out so that 15,000 Jews- every Jew still in Kraków- could be crammed into these new quarters." (Pages 76-77) How does this description set the mood for Podgórze? What kind of life should the Jews expect after moving into the new ghetto? **The description should create a mood of gloominess, desperation, and/or terror. The Jews would have realized their lives would be a lot worse.**
12. Why did the rounded stones on the walls symbolize a cemetery for the Jews living in Podgórze? **The stones resembled tombstones. The treatment of the Jews in Podgórze would most likely mean death for the Jews living there.**
13. Who shared the apartment with Leon and his family? **Mr. and Mrs. Luftig shared the apartment.**
14. What did the Nazis do after the 15,000 Jews were relocated to the ghetto? **They locked the gates.**
15. How do humans cope with extreme situations? **Answers will vary.**

Essay Question: You may have heard that stealing is never right. Do you think Leon's father had the right to steal food and coal from his workplace? Explain your answer. **Answers will vary.**

Snapshot: "If this is the worst that happens." Why would Jewish parents consider this a tool of survival? **Answers may vary. They were hoping things would not get worse for them.**

Talk About It: Why do you think the Nazi propaganda against the Jews worked so well? **Answers will vary. Propaganda is based on fears. If people fear something, they begin to hate it.**

Visualize It: Draw a picture using the description on page 76.

Chapter 5

1. Why did Mr. Luftig's pipes symbolize an orderly and civilized world? **Answers will vary. The pipes symbolized freedom. They symbolized something that could not be controlled by the Nazis.**
2. What were the causes of the rampant diseases within the ghetto? **The living conditions (overcrowded conditions and limited/no sanitation), lack of hygiene, and lack of food led to an increase in diseases among the Jews. Their bodies, starved of nutrition, could not fight the diseases.**
3. How do you think the Nazis justified their actions against the Jews? **Answers will vary.**
4. How did the Jews sustain their respect and decency toward one another? **Rabbis continued to hold services on Jewish holy days, babies were born, artists performed for the tenants of the ghetto.**
5. How did Leon spend his free time in the ghetto? **He went to Hebrew school. He played with kids his age. They performed shows. Most of the time he went looking for food to eat.**
6. How did Leon's family get money for food? **They sold Leon's father's suits.**

7. Describe how each member of the family contributed to their survival. **Tsalig repaired hot plates and other electrical items. Then he worked for a small brush-making business. Pesza worked at the electrical company outside the ghetto. Leon's mother cleaned offices.**
8. What explanation does Leon give for the reason why his family did not make plans for the future? **They were too concerned with surviving day-to-day.**
9. Explain the meaning of a "nonessential" Jew. **It basically meant any elderly or non-working Jew.**
10. What should you have inferred about Mr. Luftig leaving his pipes behind? **He knew he would not be returning. He was going to an uncivilized place.**
11. Why did the Jews react differently during the next round of evictions? **The Jews had heard from escapees about the train cars entering camps full and returning empty. The Jews had begun to realize what the evictions actually meant for them.**
12. Describe what happened to Tsalig. **Tsalig did not have a work permit. The soldiers took him away.**

Snapshot: Imagine thinking one piece of bread was a treat. What thoughts run through your mind when you think of a treat?

Talk About It: Oskar Schindler recounts seeing Tsalig. Why do you think Tsalig decided to stay with his girlfriend? What does that say about him? Do you think he made a good choice?

Chapter 6

1. What happened to Leon when he was out past curfew? **The German soldiers shot at him.**
2. Describe the conditions in the ghetto. **There was plenty of space due to the evictions. Hunger, disease, and despair enveloped the ghetto.**
3. What strategy did Leon's mother and Mrs. Bircz devise to protect them from deportation? **They would hide the children while they swept and cleaned the courtyard.**
4. Do you think their strategy was a good idea? **Answers may vary. The soldiers were beyond caring about the Jews. The strategy would probably not work.**
5. Explain why the teapot being in the courtyard was a horrible mistake? **Leon's mother had set the teapot down while she frantically tried to hide the boys. The teapot was still hot. If the soldiers noticed it, they would know there were Jews hiding.**
6. Why did they not come out of hiding after the person said it was safe to do so? **They knew it was a trick being used by the German soldiers.**
7. "Yossel and Samuel would have to rely on their own resources." (Page 105) What does Leon mean with this statement? **The boys are all alone. They have no family in the ghetto. They will need to fend for themselves.**
8. Where were Leon's father, brother and sister ordered to report? **They were told to report to Plaszów.**
9. What was significant about the orders? **It would mean the family would be separated for the first time.**
10. Why did Leon's mother push all their furniture over the balcony? **She did not want to leave anything of value for the enemy.**

11. Why was Leon pulled from the work line? **The soldier thought he was too young and small to be useful.**
12. How did Leon manage to get through the gate to Ghetto A? **When the guard at the gate was called away, Leon quickly went through the gate.**
13. What astonished Leon when he walked through the streets of Kraków? **Life was going on as if nothing horrible had been going on only a few blocks away.**
14. "Stepping through those gates was like arriving at the innermost circle of hell." (Page 112) Explain what you think Leon meant.

Snapshot: What does Leon mean when he states, "By this time survival was mostly a matter of pure luck"?

Snapshot: Explain how you feel after reading the description of Leon hiding from the soldiers. What thoughts went through your mind? Could you imagine living in constant fear?

Snapshot: Leon writes about not knowing if each day would be the last day he would see his mother. What does this make you think about?

Talk About It: Discuss what it must have been like to lose your entire family. What would you do to survive? Given the situation in the ghetto, would give up or fight for your survival?

Talk About It: How do you think the people living in Kraków were able to distance themselves to what was going on in the ghetto? Do you believe they really did not know the horrors of the ghettos?

Research It: Research Plaszów. Describe the purpose of it.

Chapter 7

1. How was Plaszów an insult to all Jews? **It had been built on two Jewish cemeteries.**
2. Describe the conditions at Plaszów. **The Jews were packed in like sardines. They were expected to do dangerous manual labor. They were counted constantly. They were fed a bowl of watery soup. They were treated as sub-human.**
3. Leon relates visiting his mother in her barracks. Why did she push him away? **If Leon had been caught in her barracks he would have been killed.**
4. Like most of the Jews, Leon's family was scattered everywhere. Explain how you would cope if you were in a similar situation. **Answers will vary.**
5. What did SS Hauptsturmführer Amon Goeth do when he visited the infirmary? **He shot all the patients.**
6. Why do you think Leon's father did not respond to Leon's story of being whipped? **Answers will vary. The answers should contain something about Leon's father feeling guilty or helpless because he wasn't able to protect his son.**
7. How did the prisoners ladling the soup make Leon's day exceptional? **They would give him a small piece of potato in his soup.**
8. Why did Leon believe he was lucky to have a job in the brush factory? **It gave him some protection.**

9. "If the next brad is crooked, I'll shoot you, he said." (Pages 126-27) What does this quote say about the character of the soldier? **Answers will vary. The soldier showed no compassion or empathy toward Leon.**
10. "I had grown numb to what might happen to me, to whatever my fate might be." (Page 127) Explain what Leon means. **He appears to be giving up.**
11. How was Schindler able to convince Goeth to build a sub-camp next to Emalia? **He manipulated Goeth into believing it would be more efficient.**
12. When Leon finds out he is to be kept at Plaszów, he states, "No words can express the absolute terror I felt. Having been given a little ray of hope, the loss of it was worse than not having had it all." What does he mean? **Answers will vary.**
13. Leon has written about the risks he has taken. Do you think the risks were worth it? Explain your answer. **Answer will vary.**
14. Why do you think the soldier allowed Leon to join the group of workers leaving for the sub-camp? **Answers will vary.**
15. What would have happened to Leon if he had stayed at Plaszów? **Answers will vary. He would have died.**

Visualize It: Using the description from pages 113-114, draw Plaszów as you see it in your mind.

Snapshot: After reading about the conditions of Plaszów, how do you think the Jews managed to retain hope? How were they able to not give up?

Snapshot: After reading about Leon's ordeal on pages 120-121, explain the emotions you found yourself thinking.

Snapshot: Imagine yourself as Leon as Goeth debated what to do with the two groups of Jews. How would your react?

Talk About It: How did soldiers justify (reason) their abhorrent treatment of other humans?

Research It: Leon describes seeing children in the Hitler Youth group. Research Hitler's Youth group. Why was it a dangerous group?

Chapter 8

1. "I knew from experience that invisibility was the closest I could get to safety." (Page 134) What does Leon mean when he talks about being invisible? **Answers will vary.**
2. Describe the differences between Emalia and Plaszów. **Guards were not permitted to enter the barracks. The food was a little better. Overall, the conditions were a little better.**
3. How did Schindler treat the Jews? **He treated them like humans. He treated them with respect.**
4. Leon writes of proudly telling Schindler he made twelve casings a night. He later found out that a skilled worker made twice as many. What does this exchange say about Schindler? **He truly was trying to save Jews.**
5. "Schindler dared to rebel against the law of the land, which was to torture and exterminate Jews, not to treat us as fellow human beings. To do that was to risk imprisonment in a labor or concentration camp or execution." (Pages 141-42) Explain why Schindler took the risks he did to protect the Jews in his factory. **Answers will vary.**

6. Why did Germany begin to lose the war? **They were fighting on too many fronts against too many countries.**
7. "When we found out German businessmen were packing their bags, leaving their factories, and fleeing Kraków with as much money as many valuables as they could carry, we knew Germany was truly losing the war." (Page 144) Why would this news not be celebrated by the Jews? **There was a risk the Germans would kill all of the Jews remaining.**
8. Why did Leon's father have faith Schindler would be able to save them? **Schindler had done it in the past.**
9. How was Leon able to save himself, his father, and his brother from being sent back to Plaszów? **He dropped the metal thermos on the ground. The noise caused Schindler to look back at Leon. Schindler was able to pull them from the group of people heading to Plaszów.**
10. Explain how the Germans were trying to hide the atrocities they had committed? **They were exhuming Jewish bodies and burning them.**

Snapshot: Leon described many incidences where a Jew's life depended on the whim of a soldier. What psychological effect would this complete control have on a person?

Snapshot: The Jews were packed into cattle cars to be sent to different camps. How does this treatment illustrate how the Germans felt about the Jews?

Talk About It: Of all of the things that happened to Leon and his family, what do you think is the worst?

Chapter 9

1. How did the accommodations at the new factory compare to Gross-Rosen? **The conditions were bad, but not as bad as at Gross-Rosen.**
2. Why was Leon's father distressed when he heard the train carrying the females had gone to Auschwitz? **Auschwitz was one of the worst concentration camps. To go there meant certain death.**
3. How did Schindler manage to get the women out of Auschwitz? **He bribed the Nazis in control at Auschwitz.**
4. Schindler spent a lot of his money trying to save the Jews. What does this say about his character? **He was kind. He has been able to retain his humanity.**
5. What was surprising about the munition factory? **Almost no ammunition was produced.**
6. How was Leon able to get scraps from the kitchen help? **He found potato peels that he then dried on the steam pipes. He also collected the remnants from the soup kettles. He was able to evaporate the water which left bits of solid food on the bottom.**
7. What affect did the transfer to day shift have on Leon? **Working the day shift was easier for Leon. The change probably saved his life.**
8. Explain why the factory workers were not optimistic about the end of the war. **The Jews had endured so much pain, humiliation, crushed hope, and loss, they did not have the energy to be optimistic.**
9. How did Schindler save the factory workers in April 1945? **Schindler managed to get the SS officer, who wanted to kill the factory workers, transferred.**
10. How did the German soldiers show themselves to be cowards? **They ran away rather than be captured by the Soviets.**

11. Why did Schindler ask the factory workers to not take revenge on the nearby town? **The people in the nearby town had help Schindler to keep the Jews alive.**

Snapshot: How do you think people can convince themselves that a group of people are less than human?

Snapshot: Why did the Jews not leave the factory?

Talk About It: Why would the Jews have a hard time comprehending the fact that they were free?

Talk About It: More than 6 million people were exterminated by the Nazis. Oskar Schindler had saved almost 1,200 Jews. Why was Schindler's accomplishment considered an extraordinary feat?

Chapter 10

1. Why did Leon want to remember the German soldiers walking past him? **He wanted to remember the defeated soldiers. They had not won. Leon had managed to survive.**
2. "Trees sprouted new leaves; wildflowers were blooming." (Page 168) What does this symbolize for Leon? **It is a symbol of rebirth. It is a symbol of a new life.**
3. How were the Jews treated when they returned to Kraków? **They were stared at with curiosity and indifference.**
4. Why did people in Kraków not welcome the Jews home? **Answers will vary. They were still anti-Semitic. Some may have been embarrassed by their actions or the actions of their countrymen.**
5. Describe the treatment of Jews in Kraków after they returned? **Rumors and lies were spreading through the city. False accusations against Jews were being made.**
6. What happened to Leon's family in Narewka? **They were murdered.**
7. What had happened to Hershel? **He was murdered.**
8. How did Wetzlar differ from the other camps Leon had been in? **There was food, medical care, and U.S. military protection.**
9. Why was it important for the Jews to have the worse story? **Answers will vary.**
10. How did Leon know Dr. Neu had retained his humanity during the war? **Dr. Neu did not pretend ignorance about what the Jews had endured during the war.**
11. What did Leon's fedora hat symbolize to him? **It symbolized his past life.**

Snapshot: What did you find startling about the number of Jews living in Kraków pre-war and after the war?

Snapshot: What, if anything, did we learn about ourselves from the events of WWII?

Talk About It: The Jews continued to be discriminated against after they returned from the camps. Do you think discrimination against a group of people still occurs?

Epilogue

1. "He had no clue of the difference between what he had experienced in having only small quantities of butter and meat during the war and what I had experienced scrounging through garbage searching for a potato peel." (Page 186) Do you think most people would have a

difficult time comprehending the hunger Leon went through during the war? Explain your answers. **Answers will vary.**

2. Explain how Leon was able to make a better life for himself in America. **He was able to learn the language, go to school, get a job, and prosper.**
3. Why did Leon flash back to the treatment of Jews after having the bus driver tell him he could not sit in the seat on the bus? **It reminded him of the discrimination he had experienced. He could not believe similar discrimination was occurring in the United States.**
4. Explain how Schindler constantly showed his humanity through his actions during the war. Use specific examples. **Answers will vary.**
5. Explain what Campbell meant when he said heroes do "the best of things in the worst of times". (Page 205)

Snapshot: Do you think it was fair of Leon to compare the two types of discrimination? Explain your answer.

Snapshot: "To many of his fellow Germans, Schindler had been a traitor to his country, a "Jew lover." (Page 196) Do you think this was a fair portrayal of Schindler? Explain your answer.

Snapshot: What would be your definition of a hero?

Talk About It: Why was it important that Leon made sure he assimilated to the ways of Americans?

Vocabulary Answers

Crossword Puzzle Answers

Across

1. making one feel inferior by belittling them
3. the act of being destroyed, made gloomy, ruin
5. hopelessness, anguish
7. Violent agitation of mind or feeling. Upheaval
9. to act boldly, blatantly, without care
10. slyly, secretly, sneakily
12. horrendous, appalling, horrifying
13. brutally, violently, cruelly
16. pointlessness, uselessness

Down

2. amazing, special, odd
4. proud, thrilled, delighted
6. impassable, solid, unforgiving
8. filthy, nasty, neglected
11. to be filled with nervousness, unease, concern
14. confusion, disorder, disruption
15. yells, screams, screeches
16. desperate, panicky, hysterical

Vocabulary Activity 1-ANSWERS

A. anxiety	F. desolation	K. furtively	P. jubilant
B. brazenly	G. despair	L. futility	Q. rampaged
C. chaos	H. extraordinary	M. horrific	R. shrieks
D. delirious	I. ferociously	N. impenetrable	S. squalid
E. demeaning	J. frantic	O. impressive	T. tumultuous

Directions: Write the letter of the vocabulary word in the space next to the correct definition.

1. making one feel inferior by belittling them ___E___
2. amazing, special, odd ___H___
3. the act of being destroyed, made gloomy, ruin ___B___
4. proud, thrilled, delighted ___P___
5. hopelessness, anguish ___G___
6. impassable, solid, unforgiving ___N___
7. Violent agitation of mind or feeling. Upheaval ___T___
8. filthy, nasty, neglected ___S___
9. to act boldly, blatantly, without care ___B___
10. to be filled with nervousness, unease, concern ___A___
11. slyly, secretly, sneakily ___K___
12. confusion, disorder, disruption ___C___
13. horrendous, appalling, horrifying ___M___
14. yells, screams, screeches ___R___
15. brutally, violently, cruelly ___I___
16. desperate, panicky, hysterical ___J___
17. pointlessness, uselessness ___L___
18. rioted, raged, charged ___Q___
19. remarkable, striking, outstanding ___O___
20. to be ecstatic, extremely happy ___D___

©2015 Jane Kotinek All Rights Reserved The Boy On The Wooden Box A Novel Study

Vocabulary Activity 2 - ANSWERS

A. anxiety	F. desolation	K. furtively	P. jubilant
B. brazenly	G. despair	L. futility	Q. rampaged
C. chaos	H. extraordinary	M. horrific	R. shrieks
D. delirious	I. ferociously	N. impenetrable	S. squalid
E. demeaning	J. frantic	O. impressive	T. tumultuous

Directions: Write the letter of the vocabulary word in the space next to the correct definition.

1. horrendous, appalling, horrifying   __M__
2. amazing, special, odd   __H__
3. slyly, secretly, sneakily   __K__
4. the act of being destroyed, made gloomy, ruin   __B__
5. proud, thrilled, delighted   __P__
6. desperate, panicky, hysterical   __J__
7. impassable, solid, unforgiving   __N__
8. Violent agitation of mind or feeling. Upheaval   __T__
9. filthy, nasty, neglected   __S__
10. to act boldly, blatantly, without care   __B__
11. to be filled with nervousness, unease, concern   __A__
12. pointlessness, uselessness   __L__
13. to be ecstatic, extremely happy   __D__
14. confusion, disorder, disruption   __C__
15. making one feel inferior by belittling them   __E__
16. yells, screams, screeches   __R__
17. brutally, violently, cruelly   __I__
18. hopelessness, anguish   __G__
19. rioted, raged, charged   __Q__
20. remarkable, striking, outstanding   __O__

©2015 Jane Kotinek All Rights Reserved The Boy On The Wooden Box A Novel Study

Assessments

The Boy On The Wooden Box Quiz 1

Chapter 1

Directions: Choose the BEST answer for each question.

1. The best description for Leon's childhood would be-
    A. innocent.
    B. horrific.
    C. terrifying.
    D. furtive.

2. Early on, Leon displays specific character traits. Which of the following would apply to Leon?
    A. Immature
    B. Childish
    C. Selfish
    D. Risk-taker

3. Leon's story begins in-
    A. The Warsaw Ghetto
    B. Germany
    C. Narewka
    D. Plaszów

4. Leon tells the reader about the relationship between Christians and Jews to-
    A. convey the hatred targeted at Jews by people of differing religions.
    B. illustrate the long-standing prejudices held by both groups.
    C. detail the prejudices held by Jews against Christians.
    D. show that Christians and Jews got along fine, other than the week before Easter.

5. One example of how Jews were treated differently in Poland would be-
    A. their inability to own a car.
    B. their inability to own land.
    C. their inability to find work.
    D. their inability to attend church services.

6. How could Leon's relationship with his grandfather best be described?
    A. Leon felt his grandfather was too pushy in his life.
    B. Leon believed his grandfather was too harsh to his father.
    C. Leon respected his grandfather immensely.
    D. Leon thought his grandfather took him for granted too often.

The Boy On The Wooden Box Quiz 1

Chapter 1

7. What happened to the men in Poland during the Great War of 1914-1918?

    A. They were forced to move to Germany.
    B. They were made to fight for the Germans.
    C. They were killed by the German soldiers.
    D. They were not allowed to return to Poland.

8. The purpose for including descriptions about his childhood was to-

    A. convey the importance of family.
    B. demonstrate that he was no different than any other child.
    C. illustrate the differences between Jews and Christians.
    D. show how anyone can have fun swimming.

9. Leon's father moved to Kraków-

    A. to work at a better job.
    B. to hide from the authorities.
    C. to escape from the Germans.
    D. to attend college.

10. The fact that it took so long for Leon's father to move his family to the city demonstrates-

    A. how little he wanted his family in the city.
    B. how hard it was to find a decent apartment in the city.
    C. how little he was paid at his work.
    D. how much he liked his freedom away from his family.

Short answer essay question: Describe the ways in which the Jews were discriminated against in Poland.

The Boy On The Wooden Box Quiz 2

Chapters 2-3

Directions: Choose the BEST answer for each question.

1. In order for Leon's family to achieve their goals, they needed to give up all of the following **except**-
   A. their father moving away from them for years.
   B. the only home they had known.
   C. their friends.
   D. their crowded city.

2. What does the word <u>extraordinary</u> mean in the following sentence? "As I pulled the chain and watched the water swish against the sides of the bowl, I thought this was about as <u>extraordinary</u> an invention as there could be." (Page 34)
   A. Disastrous
   B. Astounding
   C. Depressing
   D. Ordinary

3. What lesson does Leon learn after his teacher called him Moshe?
   A. The teacher knew Leon's father and respected him greatly.
   B. Leon learned that his teacher really like him.
   C. The teacher was very proud of Leon's work.
   D. Leon learned that the term Moshe, used by non-Jews, was an insult.

4. After reading about the Night of Broken Glass, Leon states, "In fact, much more than glass was shattered that night," the reader may infer-
   A. all Germans would mistreat the Jews.
   B. the hopes and dreams of the Jews were also destroyed.
   C. the German soldiers were also breaking in doors.
   D. the lives of Jews would go back to normal in a few days.

5. Upon seeing the German soldiers crossing the bridge, Leon states, "Although we didn't know it then, our years in hell had begun." The author most likely uses this figurative language to-
   A. create a hyperbolic image in the mind of the reader.
   B. exaggerate the situation of the Jews.
   C. compare the future lives of the Jews to a horrific place.
   D. compare the living conditions of the Jews to a familiar place.

6. "Hershel was young and strong and could travel faster than my father. At the same time, my father was rethinking his impulse to leave his wife and children." (Page 51) Based on these sentences, the reader may conclude-
   A. Hershel had the best chance of surviving against the German soldiers.
   B. Leon's father was afraid to be caught by the German soldiers.
   C. Hershel was a better traveler than his father.
   D. Leon's father missed his family.

The Boy On The Wooden Box Quiz 2

Chapters 2-3

7. The actions of the German soldiers against the Jews included all **except**-
   A. the looting of Jewish businesses.
   B. the evictions of Jews from their apartments.
   C. the cutting off of the beards and side curls of the Jewish men.
   D. the frequent attendance of prayers at the synagogues.

8. "The Poles who had pillaged our neighbors' apartment had tipped them off, telling them that we were Jews and that father had refused to hand over the key." (Page 55) This sentence demonstrates-
   A. the lengths people will go to take advantage of a situation.
   B. no one should be trusted in the Ghetto.
   C. people will go to great lengths to help others less fortunate.
   D. everyone was against the Jews.

9. "I saw the shock and shame in my father's eyes as he lay helpless in front of his wife and children." (Page 56) Why does Leon mention this example?
   A. He wanted the reader to see how dehumanizing the treatment of Jews could be.
   B. He wanted the reader to understand that not all Germans were bad people.
   C. He hoped to convey the uselessness experienced by the German soldiers.
   D. He wanted to demonstrate how the Jewish people fought against the Germans.

10. The changes in Leon's father, after his return from prison, include all of the following **except**-
    A. he lost his dignity.
    B. he lost his self-esteem.
    C. he lost his strength.
    D. he lost his will to live.

Essay Question: Explain how Leon used the stereotypes against Jews to his advantage.

The Boy On The Wooden Box Quiz 3

Chapters 4-6

Directions: Choose the BEST answer for each question.

1. Why was Leon's interactions with the German soldiers ironic?
   A. Leon was taking food from them.
   B. The German soldiers were nice to Leon.
   C. Leon bonded with the German soldiers.
   D. The German soldiers knew Leon was a Jew.

2. What can the reader infer about Leon's father from the following sentence, "When the weather turned cold, my father managed to tuck a few pieces of coal from the factory furnaces in his pockets, even though it was forbidden to take anything from the factory grounds"?
   A. Leon's father was untrustworthy.
   B. Taking care of the family was more important than following the rules.
   C. Leon's father believed he had a right to take the coal.
   D. Taking a risk and rebelling against the rules made Leon's father feel proud.

3. What does the word <u>furtively</u> mean in the following sentence? "Escapees from earlier deportations had <u>furtively</u> returned to the ghetto with stories of trains filled with people entering a camp and leaving empty, even though the population of the camp never increased." (Page 94)
   A. Openly
   B. Aggressively
   C. Secretively
   D. Adamantly

4. What do the rounded stones at Podgórze symbolize?
   A. Angels
   B. The sun (therefore, hope)
   C. Second chances
   D. Tombstones

5. "I heard a shot and then another. I felt a bullet whiz past my ear; it pierced the wall behind me. I quickly ducked into the alcove entrance of the nearest building, my heart racing. More shots rang out. Had I been hit? How would I know?" (page 98) The author uses short sentences and rhetorical questions to-
   A. convey the panic being felt by Leon.
   B. create a whimsical feeling to the exchange between Leon and the German soldiers.
   C. demonstrate how poorly the Germans were at capturing the Jews.
   D. illustrate the necessity of abiding the curfew.

The Boy On The Wooden Box Quiz 3

Chapters 4-6

6. Mr. Luftig's pipes symbolized-
   A. despair.
   B. survival.
   C. family.
   D. freedom.

7. Which of the follow was **not** an effect of the overcrowding in the ghetto?
   A. The overcrowding led to a lack of hygiene.
   B. Diseases spread quickly in the ghetto due to overcrowding.
   C. People had plenty of food to eat.
   D. Death among the Jews was frequent.

8. Leon's mother's attempt to hide herself and Leon in the rafters-
   A. demonstrated how the Jews tried to protect themselves against the German soldiers.
   B. conveyed the hopelessness of the situation.
   C. illustrated the furtive nature of Jews.
   D. showed Leon was his mother's favorite child.

9. "Yossel and Samuel would have to rely on their own resources." (Page 105) The author includes this sentences to-
   A. show how each Jew needed to fend for themselves.
   B. Illustrate how the German soldiers had destroyed anything Jewish.
   C. demonstrate how survival of the fittest was encouraged in the ghetto.
   D. convey the importance of family.

10. It was important for the author to include his observation about life outside the ghetto because-
    A. it showed how corrupt the German people were during this time period.
    B. it provided the reader with an image of daily life.
    C. it conveyed a sense of normalcy for the people.
    D. it demonstrated how people can choose to ignore what was going on around them.

Essay Question: Explain why you think the people outside the ghetto chose to ignore what was going on. Would you have ignored what was going on? Explain your answer.

The Boy On The Wooden Box Quiz 4

Chapters 7-9

Directions: Choose the BEST answer for each question.

1. A theme expressed in this story centers on-
    A. survival at any cost.
    B. be kind to others, you never know when you will need them.
    C. hope and love will solve all problems.
    D. act first, think later.

2. "At the very last moment she reached into a pile of rags on the shelf where she slept and pulled out a walnut-size piece of bread...pressed the bread into my hand, and pushed me out the door." (Page 118) The reader can infer from this sentence-
    A. Leon's mother was a thief.
    B. Leon's mother was only looking out for herself.
    C. Leon's mother was willing to sacrifice herself for Leon.
    D. Leon's mother was hoarding food to be used later for bartering.

3. "We were ordered to count the lashes as we were whipped." (Page 121) The significance of this sentence was to show the reader all of the following **except**-
    A. the strength Leon had developed during his ordeal.
    B. the importance of showing the Jews who was in charge at Plaszów.
    C. the how cruel the Germans were.
    D. the necessity for punishment in the camp.

Use the following to answer questions 4-6.

"Trying to hold it together, not yet fifteen years old, I had finally cracked. I desperately needed his sympathy, but he offered none. He showed not a flicker of emotion when I arrived or when finally blurted out my story. Instead, he remained silent, his face hardened and his jaw clenched." (Page 122)

4. His father's refusal to react to Leon's experience demonstrates-
    A. how callous his father had become.
    B. his father's inability to protect his son due to the situation.
    C. his father's displeasure at seeing his son act immaturely.
    D. his father's dislike for Leon's behavior.

5. You could best describe Leon's father as-
    A. uncaring.
    B. doting.
    C. helpless.
    D. jubilant.

The Boy On The Wooden Box Quiz 4

Chapters 7-9

6. The author included this example as a way for the reader to-
   A. understand the helplessness experienced by the Jews.
   B. imagine the daily life of young Jews in the camp.
   C. convey the urgency the Jews felt for freedom.
   D. show the lengths the German soldiers went to cause pain and suffering.

7. Which of the following describe Schindler's character best?
   A. Greedy
   B. Remorseful
   C. Selfless
   D. Materialist

8. Which of the following sentences clearly shows the cowardice of the German soldiers?
   A. Senior Nazis came through periodically and inspected our work.
   B. By that time German officers and soldiers were fleeing, doing their utmost to avoid capture by the rapidly approaching Soviet army.
   C. Next we had a "medical checkup," which consisted of our running in circles past Nazi inspectors.
   D. SS guards, as frightening as the officer who had recently grunted me into the Schindler group, stood sentry at the entrance.

9. "When I think of all his many actions as a rescuer, big and small, it is this one act that first comes to mind; I think perhaps because it demonstrates such extraordinary compassion." (Page 147) The author uses this example to explain-
   A. the depth of antagonism Leon felt toward Schindler.
   B. the complex nature that existed between Schindler and the Jews.
   C. Leon's respect and gratitude towards Schindler.
   D. Schindler's lack of empathy towards the Jews he employed.

10. "Still naked, we were assembled and processed like items of cargo." (Page 154) After reading this sentence, the reader is expected to make the following comparison-
    A. the Jews were treated like livestock on the way to the slaughterhouse.
    B. the Nazis believed the fittest would survive.
    C. the Jews were treated like animals in a zoo.
    D. the Nazis were treating the Jews like expensive merchandise.

Essay Question: After reading about the treatment of the Jews, how do you think non-Jews justified their actions (or lack of action)? Explain why those who did not agree with the treatment of Jews chose not to express their disagreement.

The Boy On The Wooden Box Comprehension Test

Directions: Choose the BEST answer for each question.

1. "Trees sprouted new leaves; wildflowers were blooming." (Page 138) What symbolism exists in this sentence?
   A. Life had gone on for everyone.
   B. A rebirth or new life was possible.
   C. The destruction from the war was being demolished.
   D. Flowers symbolized a fresh scent in the air.

2. The citizens of Kraków demonstrated all of the following **except**-
   A. they were embarrassed by their actions during the war.
   B. their feelings towards the Jews had not changed.
   C. the citizens believed the rumors about the Jews.
   D. the citizens attempted to welcome the returning Jews without prejudice.

3. The fedora hat worn by Leon symbolized-
   A. a new life in America.
   B. his past life.
   C. his childhood in Narewka.
   D. his attachment to material objects.

4. How was Leon able to overcome the hardships he experienced in Poland?
   A. He chose to forget it ever happened.
   B. He refused to talk about the events for many years.
   C. He moved to America, learned the language, and got a job.
   D. He stayed in Poland, raised a family, and carried on with life.

5. Which of the following would not be a theme of the story?
   A. Sometimes you must do whatever it takes to survive.
   B. Prejudice is an evil force that is difficult to defeat.
   C. Sacrifice is an important part of survival, including sacrificing your family.
   D. The strength to live can survive in the worst places.

6. All of the following were ways in which the German's demonstrated their prejudice against the Jews **except**-
   A. making them attend school.
   B. forcing them to relocate.
   C. depicting them as untrustworthy people.
   D. forbidding them to ride public transportation.

The Boy On The Wooden Box Comprehension Test

7. Which of these is the best summary of the story?
   A. Leon and his family sacrificed a great deal in order to survive the treatment of the Nazis.
   B. Leon and his family moved from Narewka to Kraków after his father received a job there. They were forced to move to the Poland Ghetto.
   C. Leon's family was forced to move to the Poland Ghetto after the Nazis captured Poland. The family endured much suffering at the hands of the Nazis. Eventually, Leon moved to America.
   D. After moving to Kraków and the takeover of Poland by the Nazis, Leon's family was to enduring years of hardship, discrimination, torture, and humiliation until their eventual release from a Nazi concentration camp. Leon went on to prosper in America.

8. Leon spent most of his free time in the ghetto doing the following **except**-
   A. watching movies at the local theater.
   B. foraging for food.
   C. going to Hebrew school.
   D. playing with kids his own age.

9. What lesson did Leon learn about day-to-day life?
   A. Survival was a matter of pure luck.
   B. Be nice to the soldiers because you never knew when you would need them.
   C. Sometimes the risk was worth taking if you could get food out of taking it.
   D. Respect from others had to be earned.

10. Which of the following sentences conveys Leon's feeling of being defeated?
    A. "At dawn I ate my ration of bread, returned to the barracks, and fell exhausted into my bunk."
    B. "In the span of a minute, my beloved brother was gone."
    C. "As days turned into weeks and the likelihood of finding Father deteriorated, our situation became increasingly desperate."
    D. "I had grown numb to what might happen to me, to whatever my fate might be."

11. One example of how Jews were treated differently in Poland would be-
    A. their inability to own a car.
    B. their inability to own land.
    C. their inability to find work.
    D. their inability to attend church services.

12. What happened to the men in Poland during the Great War of 1914-1918?
    A. They were forced to move to Germany.
    B. They were made to fight for the Germans.
    C. They were killed by the German soldiers.
    D. They were not allowed to return to Poland.

The Boy On The Wooden Box Comprehension Test

13. The purpose for including descriptions about his childhood was to-
    A. convey the importance of family.
    B. demonstrate that he was no different than any other child.
    C. illustrate the differences between Jews and Christians.
    D. show how anyone can have fun swimming.

14. What does the word extraordinary mean in the following sentence? "As I pulled the chain and watched the water swish against the sides of the bowl, I thought this was about as extraordinary an invention as there could be." (Page 34)
    A. Disastrous
    B. Astounding
    C. Depressing
    D. Ordinary

15. What lesson does Leon learn after his teacher called him Moshe?
    A. The teacher knew Leon's father and respected him greatly.
    B. Leon learned that his teacher really like him.
    C. The teacher was very proud of Leon's work.
    D. Leon learned that the term Moshe, used by non-Jews, was an insult.

16. After reading about the Night of Broken Glass, Leon states, "In fact, much more than glass was shattered that night," the reader may infer-
    A. all Germans would mistreat the Jews.
    B. the hopes and dreams of the Jews were also destroyed.
    C. the German soldiers were also breaking in doors.
    D. the lives of Jews would go back to normal in a few days.

17. Upon seeing the German soldiers crossing the bridge, Leon states, "Although we didn't know it then, our years in hell had begun." The author most likely uses this figurative language to-
    A. create a hyperbolic image in the mind of the reader.
    B. exaggerate the situation of the Jews.
    C. compare the future lives of the Jews to a horrific place.
    D. compare the living conditions of the Jews to a familiar place.

18. The actions of the German soldiers against the Jews included all **except**-
    A. the looting of Jewish businesses.
    B. the evictions of Jews from their apartments.
    C. the cutting off of the beards and side curls of the Jewish men.
    D. the frequent attendance of prayers at the synagogues.

The Boy On The Wooden Box Comprehension Test

19. "The Poles who had pillaged our neighbors' apartment had tipped them off, telling them that we were Jews and that father had refused to hand over the key." (Page 55) This sentence demonstrates-
    A. the lengths people will go to take advantage of a situation.
    B. no one should be trusted in the Ghetto.
    C. people will go to great lengths to help others less fortunate.
    D. everyone was against the Jews.

20. "I saw the shock and shame in my father's eyes as he lay helpless in front of his wife and children." (Page 56) Why does Leon mention this example?
    A. He wanted the reader to see how dehumanizing the treatment of Jews could be.
    B. He wanted the reader to understand that not all Germans were bad people.
    C. He hoped to convey the uselessness experienced by the German soldiers.
    D. He wanted to demonstrate how the Jewish people fought against the Germans.

21. Why was Leon's interactions with the German soldiers ironic?
    A. Leon was taking food from them.
    B. The German soldiers were nice to Leon.
    C. Leon bonded with the German soldiers.
    D. The German soldiers knew Leon was a Jew.

22. What does the word furtively mean in the following sentence? "Escapees from earlier deportations had furtively returned to the ghetto with stories of trains filled with people entering a camp and leaving empty, even though the population of the camp never increased." (Page 94)
    A. Openly
    B. Aggressively
    C. Secretively
    D. Adamantly

23. What do the rounded stones at Podgórze symbolize?
    A. Angels
    B. The sun (therefore, hope)
    C. Second chances
    D. Tombstones

24. "I heard a shot and then another. I felt a bullet whiz past my ear; it pierced the wall behind me. I quickly ducked into the alcove entrance of the nearest building, my heart racing. More shots rang out. Had I been hit? How would I know?" (page 98) The author uses short sentences and rhetorical questions to-
    A. convey the panic being felt by Leon.
    B. create a whimsical feeling to the exchange between Leon and the German soldiers.
    C. demonstrate how poorly the Germans were at capturing the Jews.
    D. illustrate the necessity of abiding the curfew.

The Boy On The Wooden Box Comprehension Test

25. A theme expressed in this story centers on-
    A. survival at any cost.
    B. be kind to others, you never know when you will need them.
    C. hope and love will solve all problems.
    D. act first, think later.

26. "At the very last moment she reached into a pile of rags on the shelf where she slept and pulled out a walnut-size piece of bread...pressed the bread into my hand, and pushed me out the door." (Page 118) The reader can infer from this sentence-
    A. Leon's mother was a thief.
    B. Leon's mother was only looking out for herself.
    C. Leon's mother was willing to sacrifice herself for Leon.
    D. Leon's mother was hoarding food to be used later for bartering.

27. Which of the following sentences clearly shows the cowardice of the German soldiers?
    A. Senior Nazis came through periodically and inspected our work.
    B. By that time German officers and soldiers were fleeing, doing their utmost to avoid capture by the rapidly approaching Soviet army.
    C. Next we had a "medical checkup," which consisted of our running in circles past Nazi inspectors.
    D. SS guards, as frightening as the officer who had recently grunted me into the Schindler group, stood sentry at the entrance.

28. "When I think of all his many actions as a rescuer, big and small, it is this one act that first comes to mind; I think perhaps because it demonstrates such extraordinary compassion." (Page 147) The author uses this example to explain-
    A. the depth of antagonism Leon felt toward Schindler.
    B. the complex nature that existed between Schindler and the Jews.
    C. Leon's respect and gratitude towards Schindler.
    D. Schindler's lack of empathy towards the Jews he employed.

29. "Still naked, we were assembled and processed like items of cargo." (Page 154) After reading this sentence, the reader is expected to make the following comparison-
    A. the Jews were treated like livestock on the way to the slaughterhouse.
    B. the Nazis believed the fittest would survive.
    C. the Jews were treated like animals in a zoo.
    D. the Nazis were treating the Jews like expensive merchandise.

30. What does the word <u>desolation</u> mean in the following sentence? "Driven by pain and <u>desolation</u>, that evening I risked additional beatings or worse by sneaking over to my father's barracks." (Page 122)
    A. Determination
    B. Misery
    C. Dedication
    D. Gloominess

The Boy On The Wooden Box Comprehension Test

Directions: Answer the following essay prompts. You should write a well-organized, thoughtful response to each prompt. Unless otherwise directed, you should write your answers on a separate piece of paper.

Essay 1: Describe how Leon changed from the beginning of the story to the end. You should concentrate on the development of his character. Provide examples that demonstrate the changes that occurred.

Essay 2: Explain whether you believe something like the events that took place during World War II could happen again. Support your answer with relevant examples (i.e. events that have taken place currently in the world).

Essay 3: Define, in your own words, the following words: prejudice, discrimination, and stereotypes. Which one is the most dangerous? Are they synonyms?

Essay 4: Are prejudices taught or innate (already within us)? Can a world really exist without some forms of discrimination, prejudice, or stereotypes?

Essay 5: Compare and contrast the discrimination experienced by Jews during World War II and a group of people today who believe they are being discriminated against.

Answers to Quizzes and Comprehension Test

Quiz 1	Quiz 3	Comprehension Test
1. A	1. B	1. B
2. D	2. B	2. D
3. C	3. C	3. B
4. D	4. D	4. C
5. B	5. A	5. C
6. C	6. D	6. A
7. B	7. C	7. D
8. A	8. A	8. A
9. B	9. A	9. A
10. C	10. D	10. D
		11. B
		12. B

Quiz 2

1. D
2. B
3. D
4. B
5. C
6. A
7. D
8. A
9. A
10. D

Quiz 4

1. A
2. C
3. D
4. B
5. C
6. A
7. C
8. B
9. C
10. A

13. A
14. B
15. D
16. B
17. C
18. D
19. A
20. A
21. B
22. C
23. D
24. A
25. A
26. C
27. A
28. A
29. D
30. B

I would like to thank the following for the use of their clip art:

Borders and background clip art:

Erin Cobb of I'm Lovin' Lit has wonderful clip art and products in her store.

https://www.teacherspayteachers.com/Store/Lovin-Lit

Pencil:

https://www.teacherspayteachers.com/Product/Time-for-School-Clip-Art-1316598

CPSIA information can be obtained
at www.ICGtesting.com
Printed in the USA
BVOW07s0822120517
483958BV00015B/60/P